Assessing Students' Written Work

Assessment is one of the most powerful tools in teaching yet it is rarely measured in effort, time and effectiveness, and it is usually done alone and against the clock. This book aims to clarify the concepts and issues that may make assessment difficult for teachers and students.

This practical and realistic book is designed to help practitioners who wish to improve their effectiveness in assessing a large and diverse range of students. It will help them to:

- clarify their role in assessment;
- gain confidence on issues and terms and consider variations between disciplines;
- compare and extend their current range of solutions to common problems with advice from practitioners;
- consider in more depth essays, reports and projects, plagiarism and language.

Both newly appointed and more experienced lecturers in further and higher education, post-graduate students, part-time staff and graduate teaching assistants will all find this an invaluable handbook and reference tool.

Catherine Haines is Assistant Director of Educational and Staff Development at Queen Mary, University of London.

NILES DISTRICT LIBRARY
NILES, MICHIGAN 49120

JUL 21 2004

Key Guides for Effective Teaching in Higher Education Series

Edited by Kate Exley

This indispensable series is aimed at new lecturers, post-graduate students who have teaching time, Graduate Teaching Assistants, part-time tutors and demonstrators, as well as experienced teaching staff who may feel it's time to review their skills in teaching and learning.

Titles in this series will provide the teacher in Higher Education with practical, realistic guidance on the various different aspects of their teaching role, which is underpinned not only by current research in the field, but also by the extensive experience of individual authors, and with a keen eye kept on the limitations and opportunities therein. By bridging a gap between academic theory and practice, all titles will provide generic guidance on teaching, learning and assessment issues which is then brought to life through the use of short illustrative examples drawn from a range of disciplines. All titles in this series will:

- represent up-to-date thinking and incorporate the use of communication and information technologies (C&IT) where appropriate;
- consider methods and approaches for teaching and learning when there is an increasing diversity in learning and a growth in student numbers;
- encourage reflexive practice and self-evaluation, and a means of developing the skills of teaching, learning and assessment;
- provide links and references to further work on the topic and research evidence where appropriate.

Titles in the series will prove invaluable whether they are used for self-study or as part of a formal induction programme on teaching in Higher Education, and will also be of relevance to teaching staff working in Further Education settings.

Other titles in this series:

Small Group Teaching
  – Kate Exley and Reg Dennick
Giving a Lecture: From Presenting to Teaching
  – Kate Exley and Reg Dennick
Using C&IT to Support Teaching
  – Paul Chin

Assessing Students' Written Work

Marking essays and reports

Catherine Haines

RoutledgeFalmer
Taylor & Francis Group

LONDON AND NEW YORK

371.272
H153a

First published 2004 by RoutledgeFalmer
11 New Fetter Lane, London EC4P 4EE

Simultaneously published in the USA and Canada
by RoutledgeFalmer
29 West 35th Street, New York, NY 10001

RoutledgeFalmer is an imprint of the Taylor & Francis Group

© 2004 Catherine Haines

Typeset in Perpetua and Bell Gothic by
Florence Production Ltd, Stoodleigh, Devon
Printed and bound in Great Britain by
TJ International Ltd, Padstow, Cornwall

All rights reserved. No part of this book may be reprinted
or reproduced or utilised in any form or by any electronic,
mechanical, or other means, now known or hereafter invented,
including photocopying and recording, or in any information
storage or retrieval system, without permission in writing
from the publishers.

British Library Cataloguing in Publication Data
A catalogue record for this book is available from the British Library

Library of Congress Cataloging in Publication Data
A catalog record for this book has been requested

ISBN 0–415–30720–1 (hbk)
ISBN 0–415–30721–X (pbk)

Contents

Illustrations

Figures

Tables

Series preface

This series of books grew out of discussions with new lecturers and part-time teachers in universities and colleges who were keen to develop their teaching skills. However, experienced colleagues may also enjoy and find merit in the books, particularly the discussions about current issues that are impacting on teaching and learning in FE and HE, e.g. Widening Participation, disability legislation and the integration of C&IT in teaching.

New lecturers may be required by their institutions to take part in teaching development programmes. This frequently involves attending workshops, investigating teaching through mini-projects and reflecting on their practice. Many teaching programmes ask participants to develop their own teaching portfolios and to provide evidence of their developing skills and understanding. Scholarship of teaching is usually an important aspect of the teaching portfolio. New teachers can be asked to consider their own approach to teaching in relation to the wider literature, research findings and theory of teaching and learning. However, when people are beginning their teaching careers a much more pressing need may be to design and deliver an effective teaching session for tomorrow. Hence the intention of this series is to provide a complementary mix of very practical teaching tips and guidance together with a strong basis and clear rationale for their use.

In many institutions the numbers of part-time and occasional teachers actually outnumber the full-time staff. Yet the provision of formal training and development for part-time teachers is more sporadic and variable across the sector. As a result, this diverse group of educators can feel isolated and left out of the updating and support offered to their full-time counterparts. Never has there been so many part-time teachers involved in the design and delivery of courses, the support and guidance of students and the monitoring and assessment of learning. The group includes the thousands of post-graduate students who work as lab demonstrators, problem class tutors, project supervisors and class teachers. The group includes clinicians, lawyers and professionals who contribute their specialist knowledge and skills to enrich the learning experience for many vocational and professional course students. The group also includes the many hourly paid and jobbing tutors who have helped full-time staff cope with the expansion and diversification of HE and FE.

Universities sometimes struggle to know how many part-time staff they employ to teach and, as a group, occasional teachers are notoriously difficult to systematically contact through university and college communication systems. Part-time and occasional teachers often have other roles and responsibilities and teaching is a small but important part of what they do each day. Many part-time tutors would not expect to undertake the full range of teaching activities of full-time staff but may well do lots of tutoring or lots of class teaching but never lecture, or supervise (or vice versa). So the series provides short practical books focusing very squarely on different teaching roles and activities. The first four books published are:

- *Small Group Teaching*
- *Giving a Lecture: From Presenting to Teaching*
- *Assessing Students' Written Work*
- *Using C&IT to Support Teaching*

The books are all very practical with detailed discussion of teaching techniques and methods but they are based upon educational theory and research findings. Articles are referenced, further readings and related web sites are given and workers in the field are quoted and acknowledged. To this end Dr George Brown has been commissioned to produce an associated web-based guide on Student Learning which can be freely accessed by readers to accompany the books and provide a substantial foundation for the teaching and assessment practices discussed and recommended in the texts.

There is much enthusiasm and support here too for the excellent work currently being carried out by the Learning and Teaching Support networks within discipline groupings (indeed, individual LTSN centres are suggested as sources of further information throughout these volumes). The need to provide part-time tutors with the realistic connections with their own disciplines is keenly felt by all the authors in the series and 'how it might work in your department' examples are given at the end of many of the activity-based chapters. However, there is no doubt some merit in sharing teaching developments across the boundaries of discipline, culture and country as many of the problems in the tertiary education sector are themselves widely shared.

UNDERLYING THEMES

The use of Computing and Information Technology (C&IT) to enrich student learning and to help manage the workload of teachers is a recurrent theme in the series. I acknowledge that not all teachers may yet have access to state-of-the-art teaching resources and facilities. However, the use of Virtual Learning Environments, e-learning provision and audio-visual presentation media is becoming increasingly widespread in universities.

The books also acknowledge and try to help new teachers respond to the growing and changing nature of the student population. Students with non-traditional educational backgrounds, international students, students who have disabilities or special needs are encouraged through the government's Widening Participation agenda to take part in Further and Higher Education. The books seek to advise teachers on current legislative requirements and offer guidance on recommended good practice in teaching diverse groups of students.

These were our goals and I and my co-authors sincerely hope these volumes prove to be a helpful resource for colleagues, both new and experienced, in HE.

Kate Exley

Acknowledgements

My thanks and acknowledgements go to all the participants I have worked with and all the students I have assessed during the past fifteen years – you have taught me many of the actions suggested within.

I particularly wish to acknowledge participants on the Post Graduate Certificate for Academic Practice at Queen Mary, University of London and all the colleagues whom I have quizzed over the past year on their approach to assessment. Acknowledgements particularly to Michelle Godwin, Sam Halliday and Ray Hall for their contributions to work on essays and projects and portfolios; to Mike Watkinson and Theo Kreouzis for comments on problem classes and practicals; to Alan Evison and Sally Mitchell in connection with the Writing in the Disciplines Project; Stephen Hibbard and Malcolm Wolfson for work at the University of Nottingham for problem class demonstrators; Sam Brenton for his advice on learning technology; Jo Longman; Kate Exley for developing much of the material and my approach for new lecturers in higher education; and Steve Ketteridge for his constructive support for the project.

I hope this will prove a useful resource.

Catherine Haines
June 2003

Introduction

This book aims to help you to cope with the many demands which assessing students' written work may make on you. It is written in response to many years of helping teachers in higher education face up to the challenges of the imperfect art of assessment – often in conditions that are far from ideal.

This book is designed to help you focus your attention where you need it most right now. We also hope you will look up chapters from time to time to improve your practice as you develop. The book is divided into two parts. Part 1, You and Assessment, focuses on your role and the skills and understanding required of assessors. Chapter 1 helps you identify your current role and to define your approach and attitude to assessment. Chapter 2 concentrates on how to assess formatively and give effective feedback to students on what they write. Chapter 3 considers the terminology and tricks of the trade of assessment. Chapter 4 examines the role of time management, planning and record-keeping in assessment practices. Part 1 closes with an examination of the generic language issues which affect all assessment of students' written work.

Part 2, You and Your Assessment in the Disciplines, applies these ideas in more detail to the different types of assessment which a beginning, part-time or occasional teacher in higher education may find themselves tackling. Will your role involve marking a mountain of laboratory reports? Will you be assessing essays set by someone else? Will you be assessing exam scripts? Perhaps you will be assessing projects, reports or dissertations? Perhaps you are assessing work aimed at developing problem-solving skills, for example, problem classes in engineering? There is a short chapter highlighting issues and practice in each of these areas.

THE SCOPE OF THIS BOOK

It is my experience that all aspects of educational practice worth considering connect with the process of education as a whole. Nowhere is this truer than with assessment. Hence the focus of this book is on how best to respond to what students write: the written products. However, is it possible to reflect on assessing an essay without also reflecting on how to teach essay writing? Is it possible to assess the product of a process without also reflecting on the process? Can content and knowledge ever be separated from the means of expression or the process of thinking that underlies it? Inevitably this book wanders into considering your role as a teacher and learner and includes many suggestions which will apply to actions you might take as a result of assessment as well as suggestions for supporting your students. My hope is that you will be able to take and apply many ideas immediately to your assessment practices but also use the experience of assessment to drive the entire learning process more effectively.

PROBLEM SCENARIOS

The approach used in this book is to pose and suggest answers to problem scenarios. These are not mere bolt-on revision sections of the text. They are based on the real-life experiences you may meet and be concerned with right now. Rather than exclusively abstract general advice which you must then re-interpret and apply, I have chosen to present many of the ideas as problems and offer suggested solutions. Glance through them. Which apply to you in some respect? Which problems can you formulate for yourself which have not been covered, or touched on? Which check-lists and habits could move you on a little in your practice? Try these, adapt them, and outgrow them.

TEN IMPORTANT IDEAS ABOUT ASSESSMENT

1 Plan the time you and your students spend assessing as if it matters – just as you plan classroom study time.

2 Make sure you understand the basic principles of assessment so you can use the tools wisely.

3 Make sure you understand your role and your approach to assessment so that you can perform your task appropriately.

4 Learn from your experience of assessing – to inform your teaching, your learning and your future assessing.

5 Everyone struggles with assessment. This is because assessment is an art not a science. We all work within checks and balances which try to minimise innate imperfections.

6 Pay attention to time management and record-keeping – it will make a lot of difference to the quality and quantity of assessment.

7 Exams require you to operate an excellent assessment technique.

8 All assessment drives student learning. Formative assessment has a major impact as well as summative grading.

9 Students struggle with predictable basics: problem solving, referencing, developing an argument in essays, imposing structure in reports and using academic language in all written work. You will often be disappointed at how long it takes students to learn things you have known for a while. It is your role to assess them so that they can improve.

10 Assessment measures achievement and can show you and your students measurable results for hard work.

Part 1

You and assessment

Chapter 1

Your role in assessment

COMMON CONCERNS IN ASSESSMENT

Listed below are questions asked by beginning teachers in Higher Education at a recent training workshop about their role and practices in assessment:

- How much detail should I give in written feedback to students?

- I'd like to know how to mark quickly, how do you do it?

- I want to know how to achieve objectivity and consistency when some aspects are excellent and others are lacking within a piece of work, i.e., how do I deal with a half model answer?

- How do I balance 'being critical' with not being too discouraging and undermining the student's confidence?

- I'd like to know about the need for marking schemes and model answers. How much should the student know?

- How do I know where to pitch the assessment and marking for Master's level work?

- How do you know whether the mark you have given is the 'right one'?

What are your key questions right now? This book aims to provide practical answers to questions like the ones above. This chapter aims to help you to clarify what your role and attitudes to assessment are right now, in order to gain the most from the relevant sections of the book. We begin with how you have been assessed.

ASSESSMENT: YOUR EXPERIENCE AND ATTITUDES

Of course, we are affected by our experiences. It is worth asking yourself a few questions about your own experience of assessment, and considering what this might mean for your style in the role of assessor.

You are, by definition, a successful product of the assessment system – or you wouldn't be invited to assess people today. It is likely that most students that you will be required to assess will have a worse assessment record than yours, have experienced less academic success and may need a different approach to encourage them to achieve their best.

 ### Some experiences of assessment: formative and summative

I remember being told at primary school not to be so stupid as to ask questions and to get on with my work. I felt this was unfair.

As soon as she said I was not very good at maths, I was determined to prove her wrong!

I was told, 'You can't do computing, you're a girl who likes English.' I did computing.

And these are just a few examples of my responses to some assessment experiences. The importance of this is that you understand your own tendencies when under pressure, and consider that the preferences and needs of others are very likely to be different.

Assessment can affect our progress

Those of us within the UK system will have passed through some common stages of assessment that have shaped our current choices. Some of these stages had direct results on what choices we had open to us. Table 1.1 shows the progression through an assessment history.

■ TABLE 1.1 An assessment history showing progression

Assessment stage	Purpose of assessment	Results	Impact on next stage
GCSE	Progression to A-level choices	A–C Pass D–F failed	Qualifies for progression
Advanced level, or GNVQ	To discriminate between candidates, i.e. rank, best to worst students.	A–F Distinction, Merit, Pass, Fail.	Directly linked to university and course of study
Access to HE, Foundation year	To provide alternative access entry for students to demonstrate their capabilities without completing previous qualifying stages	Profile of achievement samples of work	
Degree level	To discriminate between candidates	First, IIi, IIii, III, Pass/Fail	Directly linked to progression to Master's level study, some job choices
Professional qualifications for area of work, e.g.: teaching, management	To establish competence	Pass/Fail	Qualification in current job, linked to probation or promotion
Masters	To establish competence and to highlight particular distinction	Distinction, Pass, Fail	Linked to acceptance for higher study, research degree, job progression
MPhil	In arts, humanities to establish research project. In sciences, stage before PhD, or awarded instead of PhD	Pass Re-submit Fail	Linked to acceptance for higher study, research degree
PhD	To establish competence at autonomous research study	Pass Re-submit Mphil Fail	Qualifying level for academic, research positions

HOW ASSESSMENT CAN AFFECT OUR EMOTIONS AND PERFORMANCE

The best assessment experiences can motivate and encourage us to further learning and achievement and build on our strengths. The worst assessment experiences, perhaps, disappointing exam results, a failed driving test, getting lower grades than expected, can limit our life choices or discourage us from future efforts, or give us information about our limitations with respect to others.

You may have evolved preferences about the ways you like to be encouraged to work harder in your current situation; perhaps by being paid more, praised for your efforts, seeing positive results in your research. How do you want to be criticised? Throughout our working and learning lives the opinions of others about the things we are not yet doing as well as we could are of immense value. In our research work, for example, we are accustomed to seeking opinions from our colleagues, peers, supervisor, and experts in our discipline, and so on. Assessment can provide some of these opportunities for students.

Opinions on the purpose of assessment vary between the disciplines

Even the core purpose of study in your discipline can vary enormously from those of your peers in other disciplines, but tend to be consistent within disciplines. For example, which of the following, conflicting statements might be true for your discipline?

- There is no right answer.
- There is independent, scientifically reproducible truth.
- The students are here to learn to be (geographers/ historians/physicists, etc.).
- The students are here to gain a general, useful training to enable them to get a good job in the field.
- The course should provide as many real-world examples as possible.
- The course should provide a purely theoretical training in ideas for its own sake.
- The best students should all go on to study the subject at a higher level.
- The best students show daring and originality.
- Students should be here for the pure love of the subject.

- Whatever we teach them will be soon out of date, their approach to learning is of the most value.
- The best students are the most patient, accurate and disciplined; originality is inappropriate at this level of study.

Are you tough or tender?

Do you tend to assess like a hawk or a dove? Hawks like to pounce on their prey and hold mistakes up to attention and give large penalties; doves tend to be gentler and more likely to see the positives and reward them, and give higher grades to encourage a better response next time. These tendencies do not change. In other words, hawks are always hawks and doves are always doves. Within a system of assessment it is hoped that these tendencies will cancel each other out in arriving at a fair assessment, which is one reason why many assessors are needed.

HOW DO YOU SUPPORT AND CHALLENGE YOUR STUDENTS?

One of the key ideas about balancing your tendency to correct and grade people is to consider your philosophy. One suggestion is to balance the amount of support and challenge you use to assess students. If we imagine a matrix, shown in Figure 1.1, where support and challenge can be high or low, we get four quadrants with different implications for you and for your students.

Examples of supportive behaviour in assessment might be:

- Directing students to appropriate support in college, e.g. study skills and language support, tutor.
- Correcting a section of an essay for grammar, spelling and logic to show the standard you are expecting.
- Repeating information, reading, conceptual explanations, helping students review and revise material you know is difficult for them.

Examples of challenging behaviour in assessment might be:

- Making clear what the highest levels of achievement are.
- Clearly pointing out where a student is falling short of the highest standards.
- Ensuring that all students get a taste of high aspirations.

11

High Challenge High Suport			Low Support High Challenge
	High Support and High Challenge Try to reach this square in your approach!	Only the good students motivate themselves here. The rest learn that they don't like learning	
	This is often known as 'spoon-feeding'. It's a lot of work for you and it doesn't benefit the students in the long term – even if they like it in the short term	Boring for many students – and tutors	
High Support Low Challenge	Support increases		Low Support Low Challenge

FIGURE 1.1 Support and challenge in learning

SUMMARY: GOOD PRACTICE CHECK-LIST FOR ASSESSING WRITTEN WORK

1 Am I clear about my role in this assessment? (Chapter 1)

2 Do I have a clear plan for how to feedback to students in a timely and specific manner? (Chapter 2)

3 Am I clear about the definitions which apply to this assessment? (Chapter 3)

4 Am I clear about the functions of this assessment, its strengths and weaknesses and role in the course? (Chapter 3)

5 Am I clear about how I plan to use my time assessing, have I prepared an assessment sheet? (Chapter 4)

6 Do I have a clear policy on language issues? (Chapter 5)

7 Do I have a clear idea of what model answers would look like for relevant work? (Chapters 6, 7, 8, 9, 10)

8 Have I reviewed my performance and formulated ways to improve for next time?

IN THE DISCIPLINES
Your role in assessment

All the seminar plans and essay questions for the year are mapped out. I just have to select them from the departmental office and work out how to keep myself and the students interested in them. That can be hard for me when I have to repeat the same seminar three times in two days. I only see each student three times in the semester and so don't really get a chance to know them before assessing their course work.

(Tutor in Law)

I have written the whole module which is based on my area of research. I am very wrapped up in preparing for my PhD viva and find it hard to work at an appropriate level for the second years who have chosen my subject. I expect too much from them and have to take care to assess them according to the standard they are at.

(Tutor in History)

I just assess lab reports every week after demonstrating in the lab. The students are not really sure why they have to do it and don't take much notice of my comments. They only want to get the grade.

(Demonstrator in Chemistry)

I am a new sort of teaching assistant in engineering. As well as doing my PhD, I am helping to run PBL (problem-based learning) classes in the first year undergraduate module. This is only the second year of running these sorts of sessions and we are still working out the best ways to assess the students.

(Teaching assistant in Engineering)

I am one of the most experienced practitioners in our department (Occupational Therapy) and still maintain my clinical experience. I am very new to assessing written work though and need all the help I can get from my colleagues if I am to be fair to the students.

(Part-time tutor in Occupational Therapy)

PROBLEM SCENARIOS

 You know you will be doing some assessment next year for the first year undergraduates. You think it will be essays which have all been taught before. You are part-way through preparing your class time. What could you do to prepare for your role in assessment?

Request briefing

It would be a very good idea to identify who was responsible for teaching this before. Persuade them to brief you even if they are not able to hand over notes and examples; ask them questions until you are clearer about the likely pitfalls. If they are unavailable or elusive, insist that the course convenor, module leader or a senior colleague brief you.

Look at examples

Get hold of previous exam papers. If possible, ask to see examples of what would be considered typical of each degree classification and examples of the feedback expected, the style, how they report results to the office and the students. Are there feedback sheets, departmental rules on late submissions. etc.?

Compare notes with colleagues

Compare notes with your peers; get examples outside your discipline if necessary. Request to have someone moderate or co-mark your first scripts. Quiz the departmental office staff about procedures from the students' and the external examiner's points of view.

Plan your time and materials in advance

Plan your own schedule to make more time available when students will have handed in work to you for assessment. Decide on a filing system and a method for storing essays and grades effectively, set up a spread sheet perhaps; statement sheets and model answers in note form for feedback, prepare study guides/references for likely weak areas. Make sure you are clear about how support systems and study skills can help students.

Your own writing is going slowly at the moment. You are about to assess some dissertations from your students and do not feel confident in your own writing at the moment. What can you do to help?

Step back and identify your problem first

Perhaps you can try to pinpoint where you are having difficulty. Have you reached the stage of frustration? Could you make more time to enable you to focus more effectively? Are you a bit bored and stuck at the moment? Ask a peer for feedback on your writing in exchange for your feedback on their work.

Review the study skills and course material in the areas you struggle with. For example, with grammar – you could refresh your memory. Structuring? Try envisioning your work in a different way, use sticky note pads and move sections around, try spidergrams, etc. to refresh your view of the whole. Try to describe the problem exactly in detail which will help to suggest an answer.

Clarify your expectations and standards

Clarify your expectations of the level of work you are expecting from your students. Apply the level descriptors to your own work. You are likely to be operating at a higher level conceptually, in an area of new knowledge. You may also be expecting too much of yourself. Final versions are very different from the tentative, messy thinking and writing process.

Be specific in the feedback you give to students; apply the same advice to a piece of your own writing. Use it as an opportunity to learn more about the process.

You could find it really helpful as a way to develop your assessment skills on other people's writing when you reassess your own.

 You are finding that you are spending far too much time helping your students draft their projects; re-writing sections, correcting their grammar. Is there a better way?

Step back, are you helping students too much?

Perhaps you are spoon-feeding your students and offering very high levels of support and not enough challenge. Students can easily train their lecturers into this role, particularly the newer ones. Perhaps you are unclear about the limits of your responsibility and are too eager to please and they are exploiting this.

Make a new contract: what you will do, what they will do

Perhaps you can clarify your contribution from now on by agreeing a learning contract with the class. Make it clear what help you are prepared to offer to everyone. For example, you could offer one paragraph each of close corrections, but only in return for the student handing in a re-written version. Reciprocal deals tend to reduce the amount of help students ask for! You can spell out exactly what the student is responsible for (meeting the deadline, correcting spellings, etc.) and what you are responsible for.

Set yourself a time budget and stick to it

You can set stricter expectations of your time, for example, offer ten minutes per week per student only; set a final date when you will no longer offer comments on drafts. Clarify with students when their mark might be reduced to take into account the help they are given, and encourage them to seek feedback from each other.

Try not to blame the students for your mistakes in allowing them to draw you into helping. They still need some help from you and you will know better next time when and how to keep your boundaries.

FURTHER READING

Ali, L. and Graham, B. (2000) *Moving on in your Career: A Guide for Academic Researchers and Postgraduates*, London: RoutledgeFalmer.
> An opportunity to look at sample CVs of peers, with suggestions for planning and presenting your experience for your next career move, whether into a further academic post or moving on.

Allan, D. (ed.) (1996) *In at the Deep End: First Experiences of University Teaching*, Lancaster: The Unit for Innovation in Higher Education.
> An informal book which invites thirteen academics, postgraduates, and researchers to share their personal reflections about the challenges of beginning teaching in higher education.

Alred, G., Garvey, B. and Smith, R. (1998) *The Mentoring Pocketbook*, Alresford: Management Pocketbooks Ltd.
> The pocketbook series compresses some interesting concepts and suggestions into an easily digested format. They specialise in work-related skills. The pocketbooks on mentoring and negotiating both make practical suggestions which may help you establish your role more effectively.

WEB SITES

Make sure you are familiar with what the Learning and Teaching Support Network (LTSN) has to say for your areas of interest to your discipline, and the generic centre for matters of general concern and much further information about assessment. The LTSN describes itself as follows:

> The LTSN is a major network of 24 subject centres based in higher education institutions throughout the UK and a single Generic Centre. It aims to promote high quality learning and teaching through the development and transfer of good practices in all subject disciplines, and to provide a 'one-stop shop' of learning and teaching resources and information for the HE community. (http://www.ltsn.ac.uk/, accessed 23 June 2003)

The LTSN web site is www.ltsn.ac.uk

The National Postgraduate Committee runs a web site with selected articles from the press and useful links to relevant groups, unions and activities. Its web address is http://www.npc.org.uk/links

17

Chapter 2

Why and how do we assess?

INTRODUCTION

I still remember a demonstration of the power of feedback on perform-ance in a teaching course fifteen years ago. This is what happened. The pretend students were paired with pretend assessors. Students were asked to balance on one leg and stay as still as possible. Assessors were asked to ignore the results. Students had varying degrees of success and no one knew how long it should go on for. Students repeated the task. Assessors were asked to respond with mild applause. Students improved their ability to stay still. Next, students were asked to repeat the exer-cise, balancing themselves with their arms outstretched and given a target of thirty seconds. Assessors were asked to respond with an enthu-siastic round of applause. The students were able to stay still and achieve the task well.

These results suggest that with practice, encouragement, specific information about what is required, competition between peers, and reward in the form of applause, the students' performance improved dramatically. Imagine your own variations on this experiment including discouraging comments, ignoring performance, isolating students from each other and giving them unclear, contradictory information about what is expected of them, not explaining the grade or response and how these might affect the student's performance for the worse. Unfor-tunately, unless we pay particular attention when teaching, we may be guilty of carrying out some of these experiments and unwittingly reducing our students' potential performance.

The feedback that we choose to give students in all forms of atten-tion can have a dramatic effect. Remember your own response to assess-ment and feedback which you have received in the past, discussed in

Chapter 1. This aspect of assessment is one of the most powerful tools we have to motivate students and it is clearly a good idea to do it as well as we can and in more sophisticated ways than merely applauding!

THE AIMS OF GIVING FEEDBACK

The broad aims of giving feedback are:

- to encourage;

- to correct errors;

- to improve performance;

- to customise explanation for particular issues or students;

- to reward particular behaviours, for example, handing-in on time, or high standards of presentation;

- to penalise certain behaviour, for example, lateness, careless presentation;

- to demonstrate to students that tutors notice what they are doing and care enough to comment.

METHODS OF GIVING FEEDBACK TO STUDENTS

The purpose of giving feedback to students is to help them learn. They need feedback on whatever they are doing, saying or writing to help them understand whether it is right or wrong, conforms to the expected standards, is acceptable or exemplary.

A structured approach can facilitate giving of feedback. Don't just give students all the bad points, as this can be demotivating. It is important to be able to tell students exactly what is wrong in a way that lets them feel secure and see the opportunity for improvement. Likewise, you do not want to get stuck in a pattern of giving them praise without identifying areas of work that need attention. The aim should be to make the criteria clear to students so that they can judge for themselves how good their own performance is and give reasons for making that judgement.

There are two common models used to give feedback: the 'feedback sandwich' and the interactive approach.

The 'feedback sandwich'

The 'feedback sandwich' has three features:

- First strengths are identified (praise).
- Weaknesses (development needs) are identified.
- Options for improvement are explored. End on a positive note.

The interactive approach

The interactive approach aims to encourage self-assessment and reflection:

- Ask what the student thinks went well.
- Say what you (and/or other students) think went well.
- Ask what could be improved.
- Say what you (and/or other students) think could be improved.
- Discuss how the improvements could be brought about.

It is perhaps less common for an interactive approach to be used in response to student writing, and is more often used face to face. However, it is possible to combine questions which prompt the student to answer these questions when preparing to submit their work, even seeking feedback from peers to include.

Learning objectives or outcomes

In each of these cases we are assuming that the student is being given feedback on the extent to which they have succeeded in certain tasks. In order to do this, we are commonly encouraged to describe what change in behaviour we require (often called the learning objective or outcome), and how that relates to a grading or classification system (often using grade-related criteria).

A learning objective is a contract proposed to learners that describes what they will be able to do at the end of the lesson that they could not do at the beginning.

It is common practice to express the intentions from module to session level in terms of learning objectives or outcomes. QAA (Quality Assurance Agency) assessments of quality in teaching focus on these statements of what will be learned. In my view, these terms are used

TABLE 2.1 Aims to outcomes, a continuum

Term and audiences	Definition	Example
Aim ■ Public ■ Industry ■ New students	Broad and general statement of intended change of behaviour by the end of the course, or module	■ Employ scientific methods of enquiry. ■ Operate professionally as a physiotherapist.
Objective ■ Assessors ■ Teachers ■ Students ■ QAA	Specific statement from the student's point of view, of the change in behaviour. Often given at module level	■ By the end of the module students should be able to differentiate between chronic and acute pain. ■ By the end of the session students will be familiar with formulating learning objectives.
Outcome ■ Teacher ■ Assessor ■ Student	Statement which is measurable in terms of the context and range of operation and the degree of detail and accuracy	■ By the end of the session the student should be able to describe the three key features which are commonly found in Norman churches. ■ By the end of the practical, students should be able to determine three products of a mystery solution using common bench techniques.

loosely to describe a continuum of expectations, ranging from an aim, such as becoming a doctor, or being able to speak Spanish, to a specific, assessable change. The key to knowing if you are dealing with an adequate learning objective is that, if you are, it is much easier to know how to assess it appropriately. Table 2.1 shows the different stages of the move from an aim to an outcome.

What do lecturers actually write in feedback to students?

Higgins *et al.* (2000) identify broad categories of comment as shown in Table 2.2. All of these kinds of comment have a role and can be done more or less effectively and have more power and impact at different

NILES DISTRICT LIBRARY
NILES, MICHIGAN 49120

TABLE 2.2 Types of assessor comment

	Type of comment	In brief	Example
1	Regulatory instructions	'Tell them'	'Use the Harvard system of referencing rather than numbered footnotes.'
2	Advisory comments	'Better if'	'This point would benefit from including a reference to the journal literature.'
3	Descriptive observation	'This is'	'You have used 12 established sources to reference this section.'
4	Rhetorical questions	'What if?'	'How does this relate to the work of Kant? Could it be opposed?'
5	Direct criticism	'Problem here'	'A lightweight investigation of a heavyweight topic. You needed much more depth.'
6	Praise	'Praise'	'This is a well-written introduction which does its job well.'
	Correctness	Right or wrong	'This is wrong.'

stages of the writing process. One important category I wish to add is the 'simple' category of whether a fact or statement is correct or not. This is clearly very important and often shown in feedback to students as a simple tick or cross.

STUDENTS' RESPONSES TO TEACHERS' COMMENTS

We may make comments in feedback to students which follow all the rules of good practice; they may be legible, specific, timely and well intentioned. There is anecdotal evidence that students respond to comments or grades written in red with higher anxiety and hostility than to comments in other colours. The aspect we have least control over is how students may receive and interpret our comments. Spandel and Stiggins (1990) interviewed students about their interpretation of teachers' comments. Some of their findings are summarised in Table 2.3.

TABLE 2.3 Student responses to assessor comments

Teacher comment	Type	Student's response
Needs to be more concise	Advisory and critical	I thought you wanted details? Vague, vague, vague! Confusing.
Be more specific	Advisory and critical	*You* be more specific. It's going to be way too long then!
You haven't really thought this through	Criticism	How do you know what I thought? This is a mean reply.
Try harder!	Criticism	Maybe I'm trying as hard as I can! I did try! This comment makes me feel really bad and I'm frustrated.

The report concludes that:

> Negative comments, however well-intentioned they are, tend to make students feel bewildered, hurt or angry . . .
>
> What does help, however, is to point out what the writer is doing well. Positive comments build confidence and make the writer want to try again . . . comments . . . must be truthful and they must be very specific.

> (Ibid., p. 87)

This takes us back to the power of applause at the start of this chapter and suggests that important types of comment for us to make sure we increase are our use of category 6, praise, and category 3, descriptive observation. We should take greater care with category 5, direct criticism, if we want to get positive results.

FORMATIVE AND SUMMATIVE ROLES

Often we tend to blur the formative (coaching) role with the summative (judging role). It is sometimes impossible to give feedback prior to assessing (judging and assigning a grade) although there may be some scope for encouraging peers to give feedback on each other's work such as requesting plans or sections of writing for assessment rather than the whole finished product, or encouraging re-writes of the same piece rather than hoping the next piece will automatically benefit. You could decide to make extra marks available for those that choose to do this. For further suggestions see Chapter 6 on essays.

Much of the time we must do both. We are justifying a grade, pointing out errors as well as coaching for future improvements. Bean (2001) suggests adopting a consistent hierarchy of concerns, suggesting we focus on higher-order concerns before moving to lower-order concerns. Table 2.4 shows the range of possible concerns and responses.

Lower-order concerns

- Are there particular stylistic problems which you find especially annoying?
- Is the draft free of errors of expression?

Haswell (1983) advocates what he calls a 'minimal marking policy'. This could reduce your assessment time markedly and encourage autonomy and increase independent learning by your students. Consider highlighting errors in parts of the text, but not correcting or explaining each in detail.

TABLE 2.4 Higher-order concerns

No	Concern	Possible responses
1	Does the work follow the assignment?	Low grade or re-submission probable, little feedback
2	Is there a thesis or argument that addresses an appropriate problem or question?	Often becomes clearer towards the end. Commonly writer-focused, uses the piece to work out ideas rather than reader-focused in presentation
3	What is the quality of the argument itself?	Examine how it addresses the questions
4	Is it effectively organised overall?	Examine structure at macro level
5	Is the draft organised at paragraph level?	Does each paragraph have a topic sentence, that is a clear statement of a change of direction or addition to the previous paragraph subject?

Stylistic problems

Bean cites his own pet hates as lazy use of 'this' as the subject of sentences. For example, 'This practice can go on and on leading to flabby writing. This . . .'. He also penalises excessive 'nominalization'. Again, it weakens writing by turning actions into names, effectively avoiding active verbs in sentences, for example, 'transitioning into a new role'. I'm sure you have your own preferences. Students need to know how you prefer them to include quotations, references, and so on and to know that you will consistently apply preferences.

Grammar, punctuation and spelling errors

Clearly link the reduction in grade to the level of error in grammar, punctuation or spelling so that the student is motivated to find and fix such errors. If possible, describe the type of error a student repeatedly makes. For example: 'You frequently misuse apostrophes, please check this and make corrections.'

It is easy to confuse stylistic preferences with incorrect work. This is not helpful to students. Perhaps you can clearly mark errors with a cross and colour code or mark your responses in different categories.

Summarising

Bean recommends a 'strengths–major-problems–recommendations' formula. This matches the commonly used 'feedback sandwich' concept and the commendation–recommendation formula used in the examples at the end of this chapter. Including and praising specific descriptions of what the student is doing that you wish to encourage is as important as giving advice and criticism in the impact they have on future work. Focus on higher-order concerns before lower-order problems.

IN THE DISCIPLINES: EXAMPLES OF WAYS IN WHICH SOME LECTURERS GIVE FEEDBACK TO STUDENTS

Formative feedback on a portfolio of practice

Figure 2.1 is formative feedback on a portfolio of practice. This format encourages the assessor to make descriptive observations of strengths

Name of candidate: ....
Date submitted: ....
Date received: ....
Date of internal verification: ....
Name of exam board

Name of internal assessors: ....
Assessor 1: ....
Assessor 2: ....

ASSESSMENT CRITERIA

Completeness

- Introduction and cross referencing ☐   *put more context and introductory material here to help the assessor*
- Teaching observation, 2 summative, 3 peer ☐
- Mentor reference ☐
- Curriculum vitae ☐
- *I like the way you incorporate your cv into your evidence, when fully introduced and explained this could work well – almost an annotated cv.*
- Reflective commentary, 4000–6000 words ☐
- *There in essence, overall, descriptive in tone (what you have been doing) what is required is reflective, ie: why you have done it this way and how that has worked out.*
- Illustrative evidence ☐

Presentation

Getting there. You could give more help to assessors in the body of the doc. Eg. by repeating the summary of outcomes text on page 1 & 2 at the start of each section perhaps, and repeating a1 etc. in the margins.
Use of references. You need to up the no of references. Include course text, course notes and web trawl in your discipline/subject centre to bring total up to 20ish

OUTCOMES TO BE DEMONSTRATED

Cluster A: Teaching and learning in the subject

Outcome	✓ ✗	Reflective commentary: convincing/further reflection required	✓ ✗	Illustrative evidence convincing/further illustration required
A1 Deliver teaching and learning in a variety of situations appropriate to the discipline.	•	Concerned to match delivery strategy to diverse groups	•	Good range of evidence, from summer school through to post-graduate feedback

A2 Employ strategies to promote a deep approach to learning.	• Continued exploration of how to encourage greater engagement in seminars	• Useful examples provided
A3 Discuss and apply, as appropriate, theories of student learning.	• Good reflection on Kolb and others	• Aides for essay writing/ exam prep
A4 Make appropriate use of learning resources, including C&IT.	• Wide and varied range of primary sources drawn, and reflection on how to make greater use of C&IT	• Interesting evidence provided (although some photocopies not legible), and clearly made greater use of C&IT on appointment at UCL, with web ref provided
A5 Demonstrate how current research appropriate to the discipline or pedagogy, informs your teaching and learning.	• Endeavouring to make all teaching relevant and engaging	• Reading lists and egs of handouts provided
A6 Apply good practice in postgraduate research supervision.	• Reflected well on the role of the supervisor – particularly what facilitates the empowering of the supervisee	• Illustration of feedback on a chapter – extremely rigorous

Cluster A: Overall this cluster is judged to be satisfactory

Overall this portfolio is judged to be satisfactory
This portfolio is commended for the following:
- Determination – which shines through – to understand better and improve the quality of teaching, learning and assessment for students;
- The thought and application that has gone into all the sections, which suggests that Dr X is committed to continuous improvement;
- An enthusiasm and optimism that HE should work to meet the needs of ALL learners

To enhance this portfolio it is recommended that the candidate includes:
A fuller introduction to the reflective account, to provide an overview of cross-referencing – although minor by comparison to the strengths of the portfolio. I found it difficult to get into the reflective account, but once I did, aided by the portfolio of evidence, I was fine.

If not yet satisfactory, supplementary actions required by candidate:
N/A

■ **Figure 2.1** Feedback on a portfolio of academic practice

at a detailed level, objective by objective and to identify direct sections to praise. It provides an interim summary which can comment on local strengths. The summary focuses on strengths, the commendations and recommendations as advisory suggestions.

This same format is used for both formative comment on an incomplete draft as well as summatively to justify a grade. Lower-order concerns are addressed under presentation and referencing and completeness on the first page. If they are not of a high enough standard, the work has to be re-submitted.

Business management includes self-assessment

My Business Management students are required to give the following to accompany their submitted assignments:

- Three strengths displayed in this work.
- Three areas of weakness.
- How this work could be improved.
- The grade I believe it deserves.
- What I plan to pay attention to in my next piece of work.
- What I'd like your comments on.

(Business Studies lecturer)

Linking feedback with results for individuals and teams

My biological sciences first year tutor group were really struggling with writing anything at all. The idea of producing an essay seemed impossible. What I did was introduce a ten-minute writing session somewhere during the tutorial when we stopped whatever we were doing and wrote something which might be used in the next assignment. Each person reported the total number of words they wrote. I put the highest number and the group total on the board. Each week, I did the same, noting when any previous record had been broken. That's all we did. Students became much more at ease with producing text and motivated to produce more for the team.

(Biology tutor)

PROBLEM SCENARIOS

 The second piece of written work from your second years is, with a few exceptions, sloppy, poorly spelled, badly edited, constructed, referenced and presented. Where do you begin? Where do you stop?

Investigate the problem

Where a problem affects a whole group, there could be some larger problem, for example, a mismatch between the course content and the assessment, a 'log jam' of assessment which has reduced their efforts in each course. Explore issues of time management and conflict with other pieces of work set by other tutors.

It may be possible to allow the students to re-submit an edited version for an enhancement of their mark if they wish to take up the opportunity. Many will not do so and so this will not be an unnecessary burden on your assessment workload.

Feedback to the whole group

Write, or preferably get your demonstrator or research assistant to write, a model answer which you can distribute to the whole group to show what they are aiming for. Be selective and tackle the key issues first, reiterating your expectations. You may need to continue to set further tasks and exercises on one or two aspects. For example, use a set structure and reward the factual content and the standard of presentation more highly. Focus on one key aspect for subsequent sessions, feedback, tasks.

You could weight your assessment or feedback comments to reward the most important changes students need to make in each area so that students are encouraged to make widespread, if small improvements.

 The third batch of essays shows little logical progression or argument and lack of attention to referencing. You have already pointed this out several times. What do you do?

Where students are constantly ignoring an important aspect of work and taking no notice of your feedback, it may be time to change your strategy. Certainly it is not professional to give up especially when most students can fall into this category at times.

First, seek the advice of an experienced colleague. Are these essays at the expected level? If yes, try some ideas below, if not, make sure you record your concerns about the group with the appropriate module convenor. Others may agree with you. There may be other reasons such as over-assessment of students at certain times of year – everyone sets an essay in week eight, for example, and students may not have chosen your course freely, etc.

For technical issues, such as referencing, it can help to separate this skill from the larger task and set a smaller task. Get students to assess and check other people's work before handing it in to you, etc. Regarding argument and structure: this can be a mystery to many students for a long time. Again, separate the tasks, get students to present the arguments as evidence to each other, to you in the form of a plan; to summarise or précis the arguments or structure of suitable work.

 ## FURTHER READING

Newble, D. and Cannon, R. (1995) *A Handbook for Teachers in Universities and Colleges*, London: Kogan Page.
A useful little book which guides the reader through the issues which they may encounter, offering guidance in how to tackle the various issues.

Newstead, S. and Hoskins, S. (1999) 'Encouraging Student Motivation', in H. Fry, S. Ketteridge and S. Marshall (eds) *A Handbook for Teaching and Learning in Higher Education*, London: Kogan Page.
An insightful chapter on student motivation generally, with useful material demonstrating the positive effect of constructive feedback.

Race, P. and Brown, S. (1998) *The Lecturer's Toolkit*, London: Kogan Page.
A useful, quick tips approach for considering how one might give feedback to support students.

Chapter 3

What exactly is assessment?

INTRODUCTION

This chapter sets out to give some useful definitions and examples to make sure that you can play your part, whatever that is, within the assessment system. The chapter closes with a brief example of a true/false questionnaire which aims to demonstrate how concepts can be assessed using a technique which is increasingly available to lecturers, especially through Virtual Learning Environments, as well as giving you a chance to see how clear you are in your understanding of how concepts in assessment apply in your work.

DEFINITIONS

Like any professional vocabulary, educational terminology can seem vague, daunting and confusing at first. The Further reading section highlights some sources of more detailed information. So, what is assessment? Assessment is the process by which we measure the achievement and progress of the learner. Designing assessment is a skilful art because it requires the assessor to have an understanding of the content of the knowledge, the syllabus, and also the level. It requires us to judge how closely the presented work matches an ideal answer, and also the extent to which an answer falls short of the ideal, and in what respects. There is some degree of subjectivity involved as this is exercising a judgement.

KEY CONCEPTS IN ASSESSMENT

The golden rule of assessment is to ensure that assessment processes are valid, reliable and fair (Wakeford, 1999).

Validity

Validity describes the extent to which a test measures what it is supposed to measure. For example, if you were measuring somebody's height and you weighed them, it would not be a valid assessment. It would, however, be a true measure of something else, something which could be measured usefully on another occasion. For example, an assessment designed to test a doctor's skills of diagnosis would not be valid if the test measured instead the ability to carry out a certain procedure.

Reliable

An assessment is said to be reliable when it can be reproduced. For example, if the same group were to be tested twice by the same method you would expect a reliable test to give very similar results. Also, you would expect a comparable group of students at the same stage (for example, the next year's group), to achieve a very similar result on the test. An assessment must also be reliable with respect to other varying factors, such as between different assessors, the types and the choice of questions. Reliability can be said to be an expression of the consistency and precision of the test measurement. It can be mathematically determined. One way to do this is to randomly split scripts into two groups and then compare randomly chosen sub-scales. For example, for any random group the marks allocated to presentation of an essay or answers to particular question can be compared. This is known as split half reliability and should show high correlation if the test is reliable. A more sophisticated version of this idea is judged by Cronbach's alpha coefficient. This is used by finding the correlation coefficient ranging from 0, which is bad, to 1, which is perfect, giving an indication of the robustness of the rank order of candidates produced by a test.

Fair

Most of us are familiar with the concept of fairness; indeed, we are very sensitive to things we consider unfair. With respect to assessment, this means that at the very least the following conditions are met:

- There is consistency between different markers, i.e. that markers would have given similar responses and grades to any other students being assessed, and that any natural bias between different markers would be compensated for within the system.

- A marker is consistent in their assessment, avoiding bias, and marks script number 1 to the same standards as script number 101.
- There is openness and clarity between assessors and those being assessed of all the procedures and the criteria by which they are being assessed.

This means that all the assessors and assessees are aware of and have the same understanding of what is expected of them and how they will be judged. A fair system means that everyone would be in agreement about any grades awarded when they compare the results.

Fairness might mean that students have had broadly the same opportunities to study the same things in preparation for the assessment. This means students having the same amount of time, unless certain medical conditions require them to have special measures in place to make it fair. For example, this may mean providing a reader and writer for a blind student, or providing a pre-arranged amount of extra time for a dyslexic student. In the examination regulations at Queen Mary, University of London we find the following requirement:

> Dyslexic students may be granted up to fifteen minutes additional time per hour in written examinations (the norm is ten minutes): the time allowed is based on the report of an independent educational psychologist. In addition, the scripts of dyslexic students will be flagged and each Exam Board has been asked to determine a procedure for considering such scripts which has regard to the students' difficulties with the use of words and sentence structure.

Standards

We have all heard complaints of standards falling in our education system. The standard is used to refer to student attainment in terms of what was expected and what was actually achieved. For example, an excellent student who achieved a poor grade in a piece of work would be said to have a lower standard than was usual for them. When cohorts all achieve results which are above the expectations of previous years, we might say that the standard across the board has risen.

Plagiarism

It is important that tutors help students be clear about how plagiarism is defined in their context. There will be many occasions when you are inviting students to cooperate and collaborate and produce joint work, including incorporating feedback and ideas which others have contributed to discussion. The borderline between this and collusion, presenting other people's work as one's own, can be subtle. Students may need you to reinforce this boundary clearly with them to ensure that they are not contravening a legal boundary as well as a cultural one.

Within their individual work, students can also benefit from clear guidance about how to incorporate the ideas they are working with in published text. This is good practice in developing skills of academic writing and much plagiarism is accidental and reveals more perhaps about our failure to instil skills of academic discourse in our students than their wilful cheating. In scientific subjects, the integrity of the scientific method itself can be jeopardised by cheating. There are important historical examples where such cheating has damaged the progression of science which may help to show students why this is so important.

Poor assessment invites plagiarism. If students are asked to do the same tasks year after year, if the main aim is to obtain a grade, if the assignments are very similar to lots of other assignments and are subject to minimal supervision or face-to-face contact, then the chance of plagiarism may increase.

The Joint Information Systems Committee (JISC) has launched a plagiarism advisory service. This service provides online access to a variety of information, including generic guidance on issues relating to plagiarism. This service is free but requires institutions to register by signing a use agreement. This and further details of JISC project work can be found at: http://www.jisc.ac.uk/mle/plagiarism

Useful services for tutors are likely to include:

- Recommendations on assisting student learning of study skills and essay writing, which, it is hoped, will be accompanied by learning tools for students on avoiding plagiarism.
- Case studies.
- Guidelines on processing assignments.
- Plagiarism detection tools.

If you let students know that you are prepared to run suspect text through plagiarism detection software, this will act as a deterrent. There is a review of plagiarism detection sites at http://www.coastal.edu/library/mills3.htm. Even a widely available search engine such as google is able to identify close matches to sections of text and some tutors find this sufficient.

TYPES OR MODES OF ASSESSMENT

Formative assessment

Formative assessment is assessment that is used to help teachers and learners gauge the strengths and weaknesses of the learner's performance while there is still time to take action for improvement. Typically it is expressed in words rather than marks or grades. Information about a learner is used diagnostically. For example, in some courses no first year assessments are put towards the classification of the final degree. The assessments are just pass or fail (summative element), however, grade information and feedback are often supplied to enhance the learning of the student and help tailor the teaching to the needs of the group.

Continuous assessment

Continuous assessment is when course work throughout the term is assessed and counts towards the final summative assessment. Courses vary in the proportion of continuous assessment which they can allow, with some disciplines excluding traditional unseen examinations altogether in favour of continuous assessment. This can be seen as a better test of performance over a sustained period of study rather than an exam. Many courses now include a proportion of course work towards the summative grade. In some schemes it is possible to require students to select the top few assessed pieces of work to go forward to be counted summatively, to provide a little flexibility to the continuity and allow for the occasional lapse in standard of work.

Summative assessment

This type of assessment typically comes at the end of a section of learning and awards the learner a final mark or grade for that section. The information about the learner is often used by third parties to inform decisions about the learner's abilities.

Summative assessment is usually the most feared type of assessment from the student perspective as it has implications for further study and life choices and determines this degree classification. This type of assessment is often subject to the most wide-ranging methods to try and ensure validity, reliability and fairness. For example, setting exam questions will be subject to many procedures. Dissertations, coursework, projects may all be subject to checks such as double marking and external examining in order to ensure best practice.

Example: College marking and grading scales at Queen Mary, University of London

Unit marking scale		Honours Degree classification
> = 70	A	I
< 70–60	B	IIi
< 60–50	C	IIii
< 50–45	D	III
< 45–40	E	Pass
< 40	F	Fail

Criterion-referenced assessment

This type of assessment judges how well a learner has performed in comparison with a pre-determined set of criteria, or statements about what a student might be expected to be able to do at that level, in response to that assessment. The QAA subject benchmarks are written as criteria identifying achievements commensurate with different levels of performance. Criteria can be set to pass or fail, as in a professional course designed to develop and ensure that those completing it are competent at their job, for example, lecturers in higher education. There can also be grade-related criteria, where different levels of attainment are spelled out so that it is clear what is required for a fail, a pass, a third class, or a lower second class degree.

Here are some comments about the use of assessment criteria for Undergraduate Geography at Royal Holloway, University of London.

The following assessment criteria are intended both for the use of staff in marking work within the Department and to allow students to see the general criteria that are used to calculate grades. The assessment criteria give general models of the characteristics that are expected of work being awarded particular grades. The following points should be borne in mind in their use:

- These criteria can only be indicative, and many pieces of work will have characteristics that fall between two or more classes. Examiners retain the ultimate decision as to the mark given to a particular piece of work. The assessment criteria provide a useful basis for discussion between examiners.
- These criteria give general models of assessment criteria. They do not remove the need for course leaders to give clear training and written indications of the specific criteria required for success in specific courses.
- These assessment criteria have been designed to comply with the general standards for threshold and typical standards set out in the QAA Geography Benchmarking Statement.

It has been known for some teachers to be reluctant to spell out exactly what would be required as if this represents some form of 'cheating' or makes the task easier. Of course, in a right/wrong subject, answer criteria may still have something to add.

Levels of assessment

Criteria also need to relate to the level of attainment expected at a particular level. Clearly, the first class answer for a year one essay might be expected to be at a lower level than a first class answer at the end of the third year. Similarly, a Master's level dissertation would be assessed at a different level from a first year project. For a degree qualification is would be necessary to demonstrate success at a number of levels, appropriate to the progression through the course. Institutions can describe these assumptions in different ways and degrees of specificity. One consortium of universities, the South Eastern England Consortium (SEEC), has published generic guidelines to accompany criteria and outcomes at different levels and can assist in interpreting what is implicit and explicit within your system where this is not already locally defined.

Many assessors report being able to identify first or third class work relatively easily. In other words, the extremes of the scale are clearer. However, for candidates (most of them) who tend towards the average, it can be harder to demonstrate agreement. Where grades fall at the borderlines between categories, the final class may depend on how the results and criteria are interpreted by the exam board.

Interpreting supposedly factual evidence

Depending on the discipline and implicit criteria being used to mark the same sum, it can be demonstrated that there would still be a variation of marks. For example, a civil engineer might argue that anything less than a 100 per cent correct answer should lead to a zero score because in the context in which the engineer is working it would make the difference between a bridge standing and collapsing and killing people. A mathematician might give almost full marks, arguing that by their criteria 99 per cent of the mathematical operations had been performed correctly and so deserved a high grade.

Through this example I hope you can see that whether you spell them out or not you are actively constructing and operating by complex rules and criteria whenever you judge or assess. When you are developing your teaching skills, working within a new department, operating on a cross-disciplinary course, or a different institution, in each case it is important for fairness, validity and reliability that teachers actively construct their understanding and operation of criteria for their judgements. Colleagues who may have been doing this for many years may not need to write them down clearly in order to use them, however, external agencies, new and other colleagues and especially the students will benefit enormously from being able to work with the same set of statements describing the complex business they are involved in.

Transparency

This term is often used to describe a desirable situation when all the criteria for success are clear and known to both staff and students and when the assessment procedures and protocols can be tracked by the external examining system.

Norm-referenced assessment

Norm-referenced assessment judges how well a learner has done in comparison with the performance of their peers. For example a professional accountancy or law exam may have a pre-determined number of candidates who can pass which is set before the exam is taken, let's say, 40 per cent. For each cohort it is theoretically possible for people to pass who may have failed if their performance had been measured against a different set of peers in a bad year or to fail if their score was in the lower 60 per cent of a group of peers in a particularly good year.

In recent times the UK education system has been tending to move from a norm-referenced system for public examinations such as A levels towards a criterion-based system of assessment. This can mean that it may appear that standards have gone up and more people do well because they and their teachers and their examiners are clearer about what is required. It may also appear that standards have fallen because more people have achieved a higher score, therefore the exam must have been easier.

ROLES IN ASSESSMENT

External examiner

External examiners are part of universities' self-regulatory procedures and play a key role in maintaining standards between institutions in a particular discipline. Usually distinguished members of the profession who have the respect of colleagues and students alike, for taught courses they typically act for a defined number of years – often three. External examiner reports form the basis of institutional review of courses and programmes for quality assurance purposes. They play a similar role in the examination of postgraduate dissertations and theses and lead in discussion in viva voce examinations.

Externals address their reports directly to the Principal or Vice Chancellor of an institution. The system is designed to provide an informed, disinterested third party who is free to make a judgement about the standards of one institution relative to their own institution and their knowledge of the sector. Examiners will view samples of work from students attaining different grades within the course and often meet and informally discuss the experience of the course with students. This allows them to build as impartial a view as possible of the achievements of the course. External examiners can often help a course team take a difficult decision, such as failing somebody, without the personal involvement that the lecturers will have built up.

Similarly, they can recommend that different summative assessments are awarded if they believe the grading is too stringent relative to the standards of the sector, or too lax. They are also in a unique position to be able to document particular issues concerning students and staff, resources, difficulties and successes, directly to the top of the institution. Current trends in accountability are beginning to recommend that these reports are made public to assist in students and funders deciding between courses. Maintaining a balance in a constructive relationship between a course team and an external examiner can be difficult.

A key task of the external would be to sample coursework and criticise the examination questions which will be set for students in advance. It is likely that you might be required to participate in these activities, and have to prepare documentation for submission to the external. Examiners get paid a nominal fee for this work and consequently their time is often well programmed during short annual visits, so you may not meet one for a while – but you will almost certainly be documenting and participating in procedures which they will examine.

Moderator

This is the name for the person who carries out the process of comparing assessed work and the results of various different assessors and processes to ensure that the summative grade awarded is fair. In some systems of assessment this name is given to the external examiner; in others this process is described as internal or external verification. At Queen Mary, external examiners have the right to examine any script or other assessed material. Their role is to moderate, or to compare their calibration of what constitutes a first with that of the internal examiners. If there is a significant alteration to the mark for scripts, the relevant examiners consider whether the marks for the whole cohort should be reviewed.

TECHNIQUES IN ASSESSMENT

Blind marking or double blind marking

Blind marking is the process when two separate assessors mark a piece of work and award a grade independently, before they are aware of the decision of the other assessor. Assessors can then 'moderate' their judgements if necessary. This is often how less experienced assessors will begin assessing, comparing their work with a more experienced assessor. Obviously, this doubles the amount of assessor time and so is usually reserved for substantial pieces of work, such as a thesis or project and work which counts towards degree classification. It is also useful for assessing highly subjective work such as studio, design and performance work.

Double marking

Here two assessors mark one piece of work. However, this need not be blind. For example, there could be a first or lead assessor who assesses first, a second assessor could then more quickly track the assessment decisions and grades of the first assessor and then raise any anomalies for moderation. It is possible for samples of an assessment to be double marked, for example, one in ten essays or exam questions.

Sampling

When a lecturer chooses to re-mark a representative proportion of student work (either one question from some scripts, or a proportion of whole scripts), they are using sampling techniques to assure the reliability of their own assessment. This is a relatively straightforward way to check one's own assessment in a minimum amount of time and can be very useful.

Assessing equivalence

Obviously each project, thesis, dissertation, survey, design, experiment, and piece of art is different. Some appear to be easier, less demanding and some may prove much more challenging. How can assessment be fair in these circumstances? Just as equal opportunity is often misunderstood and thought to mean that everything has to be the same to be fair, it is possible, with effort, to ensure that students have an equal opportunity to succeed even if the tasks are not identical. It is important that the assessment criteria are designed to ensure that all students will have an equal chance of gaining a high mark.

41

SOME NEWER ASSESSMENT METHODS

Portfolios

A portfolio is a carrying case for drawings and designs of things which cannot be carried about, like buildings, or designs for things which have not yet been built. Portfolios enable people to see and assess the range of achievements more easily. In recent years, this idea has been extended to include electronic media, for example, video tapes of performances, talks given, installations and electronic references. Portfolios are commonly used to assess work in art, design, architecture as well as in professional practice courses, such as teaching, counselling and social work.

The NVQC (National Vocational Qualifications Council) has been developing a process in collaboration with industry lead bodies over the past decade or so which can assess every task in the workplace. Portfolios have been used to present evidence of their achievements. Professional qualifications have adapted these ideas or developed them from their chartership schemes and commonly are assessed using portfolios. Schools encourage pupils to document their progress using a National Record of Achievement. Doctors and nurses show how they have remained up to date and fit to practise through submitting portfolios to their professional bodies. Essentially, a portfolio is a special selection of evidence documenting achievements for the purpose of assessment, usually against a set of criteria or outcomes.

Portfolios encourage the pass mark for a course to be considered at 100 per cent; a level far in excess of that required for most other types of assessment – for example, exam pass marks are often 45 per cent for undergraduates or 40 per cent at postgraduate level.

Computer-assisted assessment (CAA)

The term encompasses the use of computers to deliver, mark and analyse assignments or examinations. It also includes the collation and analysis of data gathered from optical mark readers (OMRs).

Computer-based assessment (CBA)

A computer-based assessment is one in which the questions or task are delivered to a student via a computer terminal. In most cases the student's answers are typed in at the computer keyboard and recorded and marked electronically.

There are many pedagogical advantages to using CAA. First, CAA can enhance formative and diagnostic assessment:

- Students can repeat formative assessment as often as they like.
- Tests can adapt to student ability, for example, providing clues.
- Detailed feedback is available immediately.
- More frequent assessment of students is made possible by the automatic marking of scripts.

There are also administrative advantages:

- Marking is not as prone to human error.
- Computerised marking saves staff time.
- Large groups can be assessed quickly.
- Diagnostic reports and analyses can be generated quickly, in time to affect the teaching.
- Grades can be automatically entered into information management systems and student records databases.
- Can reduce cheating through randomisation of questions.
- Eliminates the need for double marking.

CAA is limited, chiefly because implementing a system can be costly and time-consuming, including monitoring the hardware and software to avoid failure during exams. Students also require adequate IT skills and experience of the assessment type. It requires skill and practice to construct good objective tests which will assess higher order skills and knowledge. Assessors and invigilators need training in assessment design, IT skills and examinations management. Providing a valid, fair and reliable assessment system using computer-based assessment therefore requires a high level of coordinated organisation between academics, support staff, computer services, quality assurance and administrative staff.

Although recent studies have shown that there is a bias towards science and technology subjects at this stage, there are increasing examples of the use of CAA in other disciplines. See Further reading at the end of this chapter.

Virtual Learning Environments (VLEs)

A Virtual Learning Environment is a computer-based system which aims to provide an integrated experience of learning which can meet the individual needs of the teacher, assessor, student, administrator, to describe, deliver and record the learning of a course. In recent years, Virtual Learning Environments have included increasingly sophisticated tools for CAA. For example, with WebCT (one package which is in use in HE), tutors can design multiple choice questions, yes/no questions, short answer, and essay questions which the student takes online. The tutor can include feedback to specific questions and answers, can choose whether the test can be retaken, when it is released and when it expires. The results can then be analysed.

Self-assessment

Self-assessment is increasingly being included in the range of assessment techniques in order to develop the students' own powers of judgement and discrimination. It usually invites the student to submit their own account of their strengths and weaknesses with an assessment, and sometimes to give their response to the assessor's judgement. More rarely, students can allocate their own grades (summative assessment) or have their self-assessment moderated by the assessor and if the assessor agrees, to stand as the grade.

Peer assessment

Peer assessment is increasingly involved in providing opportunities for students to gain feedback on their work from sources other than just the academic staff. This is particularly important in times of larger class sizes and pressures on staff time. However, it also has the benefit of contributing to the student learning process by familiarising the student with issues of judgement and the criteria by which they are being assessed. This is perhaps easiest to include as a source of formative feedback, but could also be moderated by the assessor as above.

When writing intensive courses, or courses developing professional practice, it can be very successful to require students to seek feedback from a peer on their practice, or on drafts of written work and submit them as part of the assessment process.

SUMMARY OF FEATURES OF GOOD ASSESSMENT

■ Clarity about the purposes of assessment (e.g. to discriminate between strong and weak students).

■ Consistency to all candidates of task, marking, grade, etc.

■ Free of bias (application of equal opportunities – culture, language, gender, age, disability).

■ Double/multiple marking in summative assessment (reliable/fair).

■ Blind marking (summative) assessment (fair).

■ Criteria for success (content and level) known to staff and students (transparent).

■ Moderation by external examiners of assessment which counts.

■ Appropriate in terms of amount.

■ Opportunities for feedback to students, especially on formative assessment.

■ Assessment content and appropriateness of task to judge students' achievements against stated goals (valid).

■ Varied (i.e. in type to give opportunities for different students to demonstrate their strengths).

■ Assurance that all markers conform to grade criteria, model answers, etc. (reliable/fair).

■ Accurate and appropriate records kept.

■ Adherence to college and university regulations.

■ Clear procedures for appeal.

■ Where applicable, conform to standard for a particular profession.

TRUE OR FALSE

Which of the following statements are true?

1 Formative and summative assessment can never be combined in the same assessment.

2 An external examiner can:
   (a) Alter the marks of an individual student.
   (b) Make sure the process is completely fair.
   (c) Question the validity of your exam questions.

3 A portfolio is:
   (a) A straightforward way of assessing content recall.
   (b) A useful way of including personal and reflective deep learning in a professional training.

4 Essay writing skills can be improved by:
   (a) Giving more time to write them.
   (b) Getting feedback on essay plans.
   (c) Getting students to assess essays.

5 An exam where only 40 per cent of candidates can pass is an example of:
   (a) A criterion-referenced approach.
   (b) A stringent standard.
   (c) A blueprinted assessment.
   (d) A norm-referenced approach.

6 A portfolio can achieve 100 per cent if it is good enough.

7 Blind marking influences grading.

8 Double-blind marking is the only method of ensuring fairness.

9 Multiple choice questions tests can only test content.

10 Essays are the only way to test higher order skills in the humanities.

Suggested answers

1 False. Assessments often include elements of both.
2 (a), (c)
3 (b)
4 (b), (c)
5 (d)
6 False, or extremely unlikely.
7 True. It can help to eliminate bias, conscious and unconscious.
8 False.
9 False.
10 False.

 FURTHER READING

Brown, G., Bull, J. and Pendlebury, M. (1997) *Assessing Student Learning in Higher Education*, London: Routledge.
A useful book which provides a more detailed discussion of assessment.

Entwistle, N. *et al.* (1992) 'Guidelines for Promoting Effective Learning in Higher Education', *Assessment*, Edinburgh: Centre for Research on Learning and Instruction, University of Edinburgh.

Gibbs, G. *et al.* (1986) *53 Interesting Ways to Assess Your Students*, Bristol: Technical and Educational Services.

Wakeford, R. (1999) 'Principles of Assessment', in H. Fry, S. Ketteridge and S. Marshall (eds) *A Handbook for Teaching and Learning in Higher Education*, London: Kogan Page.

 USEFUL WEB RESOURCES

CAA Unite at Loughborough http://www.lboro.ac.uk/service/ltd/licaa/index.html

SCAAN (Scottish Computer-Assisted Assessment Network http://scaan.ac.uk Subject specific links can be found at the CAA project site, closed in 2002, but the site is preserved.

http://www.caacentre.ac.uk/resources/web/ikndex.shtml

http://www.ltsn.ac.uk/application.asp?app=resources.asp&process=full_record&section=generic&id=7
A download publication which refreshes your understanding of assessment terminology produced by LTSN (Learning and Teaching Subject Network) as part of their assessment series.

http://www.ltsn.ac.uk/genericcentre/asshe/

JISC (Joint Information Strategy Committee) online plagiarism advisory service http://online.northumbria.ac.uk/faculties/art/information_studies/ Imri/JISCPAS/site/jiscpas.asp

QAA (Quality Assurance Agency) guidelines on external examinations available at: http://www.qaa.ac.uk/public/cop/copee/appendix1.htm accessed on 23 June 2003

MCQ software: CALnet: http://www.webecon.bris.ac.uk/calnet/

QuestionMark: http://qmark.com/uki/home.htm

TRIADS: http://www.derby.ac.uk/assess/talk/quicdemon.html

CASTLE: http://www.le.ac.uk/castle/ikndex.html

Respondus (for designing MCQ tests to then export to a VLE) http://www.respondus.com

Chapter 4

Time management

INTRODUCTION

Many of the tips which experienced assessors have to pass on are to do with time management and managing all the paperwork associated with assessment. When we have been doing a task for a long time we are able to refine and improve a system and find the shortcuts. This chapter attempts to pass some of these tips on to you without you having to work them out for yourself.

Time is our most precious resource. Current systems for measuring teaching and learning effort seldom measure the time students spend preparing for assessment and teachers take carrying out those assessments. This is territory ripe for you to do your own time and motion studies. Theoretically, we all have the same amount of time available to us each week: clearly, people achieve different results with the same resource.

 TEN CRUCIAL TIPS FOR MANAGING TIME AND INFORMATION IN ASSESSMENT

1 Time spent planning and preparing will reduce the time you spend overall on assessment.

2 Being aware of how you use your time can reduce your stress levels.

3 Individuals tend to have different patterns of concentration and preferences for working: understand and harness your own.

4   Seek simple ways of doing things; these are the easiest systems to maintain, but sometimes the hardest to invent.

5   Make use of technology to save time and to automate labour-intensive parts of the process but do not unnecessarily complicate the process.

6   Assessment requires good concentration, good methods, and often a large slice of time, therefore it is prone to being delayed, interrupted and in conflict with your other tasks, research and social life.

7   Assessment often takes place in annual cycles dictated by the needs of others. You can predict and plan your other activities around this.

8   Assessment scripts and records are very important documents and your systems need to be robust enough to preserve their security and integrity.

9   Many assessment tasks are actually clerical: organise yourself well and you can focus on your real contribution – academic judgement.

10 Mistakes in assessment are professionally embarrassing and yet hard to avoid without effort. It's worth investing some time here.

KEY IDEAS IN TIME MANAGEMENT

There are many books on this subject some of which are listed in the Further reading at the end of this chapter, but there are some crucial concepts I wish to focus on.

Not all time is the same

As human beings with circadian (daily) energy rhythms, appetites, seasonal changes and so on we are better matched to carry out some tasks at particular times. Are you someone whose best time is early in the morning? Late at night? Weekdays only?

Best time perhaps can be conceived of as when most mental energy is available for achieving the current task. It makes sense to realise when our own personal best times are and to schedule our creative and important work for these times. For example, I find that my most creative working slots during the day are for the first hour and a half of the day, when I am at my freshest, and again in the late afternoon, when I can suddenly find focus and concentration to achieve a great deal of what felt impossible straight after lunch. Incidentally, some educational systems feel so strongly about the physical evidence for such changes in our ability to concentrate that they timetable all school cognitive subjects in the morning. Anyone who gives a lecture at 9 a.m. on a Monday morning or on a Friday afternoon, after lunch, will know that in order to motivate their students they need to employ as many motivational, stimulating tactics as possible in order to keep the students focused.

It seems sensible that at least some of your assessment time could benefit from being scheduled to your best time for working; a great deal of preparation and straightforward assessing can then be done in your average time.

Time management by routines and cycles

Some people deal with their time management by creating habits and routines which allow them to fulfil the tasks they have to do. For example, you could decide that because you prefer to work uninterrupted, you will do your assessment at home each Thursday afternoon. Your routine could be to use a set amount of time every week working towards your assessment tasks. Sometimes there will be lulls between assessment and when this time is still allocated to assessment, perhaps to planning and preparing for future assessment in order to keep the routine and good habits in place. A routine has the advantage of not inviting you to vary and change your work habits based on how you happen to feel on a particular day and helps large tasks remain manageable and never be overwhelming. There may well be many among you who rebel at the very idea of using such set routines to work; you came into academia to avoid the crushing routine of a set workload. I can empathise. However, whether we intend to or not, human beings are pattern making, habit-forming animals. It may be that you can improve the habits you have fallen into.

As well as daily routine, academic life is mostly strongly obedient to weekly, termly, semester and annual cycles. In some ways, each week is different and it may be at least a year and maybe more until the

51

assessment task comes round again in a similar form. Much of this can be predicted. In the same way as you would encourage your students to plan ahead to ensure they have exam time and revision time well organised, there may be benefits for ourselves in a similar approach. A chart where your workload for assessment will fall in the year might reveal when you may be able to prepare and minimise peaks and troughs in your assessment workload. With exam boards, it is particularly important to plan backwards from the fixed date and include contingency time for unseen problems and delays.

Categories of time: sold, balanced and demand-free time

Broadly speaking, we get three choices as to what to do with our time; interestingly, two of them are not really choices at all. Customarily we sell some of our time in order to make a living. Let's call this category, sold time. It contains all the tasks which are necessary for us to retain and even excel in our job. This might include commuting to work, preparing for teaching, doing research and many things which may not be done actually in work time actually on work premises, but where we are not available to spend time in the other categories.

The next category might be termed balance time. This category of activity includes all those tasks which is necessary to maintain ourselves as a healthy, well-balanced human being. For example, we don't really have much choice over whether we want to shop and prepare food, mend and clean our homes. However, this category also includes important social relationships, such as visiting your friends and family, being active in the community, participating in your religion, improving your fitness by going to the gym, managing your stress by doing yoga, even ensuring you relax sufficiently to function well. We may often consider activities such as watching a film, eating out with friends, or going on holiday as optional extras, however, the consequences if we do not relax sufficiently can be serious.

Anything that is left might be considered as truly free time. This is time over which you have sole control, it is not strictly necessary in order to keep your body and soul together; it is yours to choose how to spend. In some ways this is very creative time where life can be actively experienced and enjoyed and where good ideas can come from. One surprise here is that we tend to imagine that there is much more of this resource than a balanced life allows. It makes sense to me to be clear about when this time occurs and to be really clear about what I want to do with it, free from immediate demands.

In the short term, many people deal with these categories of time by letting them blend and borrow from each other. For example, if you have lots of essays to mark, you may skip going to the gym, or even seeing your friends. You may be new to your work role and keen to put in the extra hours which will allow you to demonstrate your capabilities. You would be borrowing from your balance time to extend your sold time. If you don't arrange to 'pay this overdraft' back later, perhaps with a holiday, you may get further out of balance, stressed and even ill. A life without time which is free of immediate demands can become a little stale and repetitive in the long term and can stifle creativity.

Rewarding yourself

One stage which is neglected in time management is to ensure that you have ample and richly enjoyable systems for rewarding yourself! Most of our rewards from external sources, bosses, colleagues, academic peers, the Nobel Prize committee, are few and far between. It is very human and necessary for us to design and enforce regular enjoyable rewarding habits. This is what we are doing when we seek a chat with someone, get a cup of coffee, have a biscuit, whatever. What is enjoyable and rewarding for you? Do you enjoy a short walk, a day-dream, a snooze, a chat, an email to a friend, a quick browse on the Internet, a bit of thinking, a break for lunch or coffee, a trip to the bookshop? Whatever is available to you in your working day that you feel is a treat and a reward; make sure you regularly reward yourself with enjoying it in between your tasks. It might make sense to bring back some of those old habits – joint tea breaks when everyone could have a chat at the same time. You don't want to become part of someone else's reward system when you are deep in your best time of day. Share ideas with others. Think creatively.

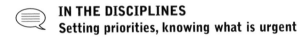

IN THE DISCIPLINES
Setting priorities, knowing what is urgent

I find it so easy to fill the week being busy and feel I have got nowhere, so I have a list of the ten most important areas of my life at the front

53

of my diary. Each week I set myself a target in each area. It really helps me to feel I am moving towards my long-term goals.

(Biological Sciences demonstrator)

I keep a picture above my desk from a time management course I went on. It shows a grid with four slots; urgent and important, not urgent and important, and urgent and not important and neither urgent nor important. When I remember, I ask myself if I've done anything today which is important and not yet urgent . . . that's where my research and ideas need to come from and where it's easy to neglect.

(Business Management tutor)

 ## Some paper management suggestions

I set up slots labelled with days of the week in my filing cabinet. When I've prepared some work which I'll need to use on a particular day, I put it in the slot for that day. At the start of each day, I sort things out in a folder so I deal only with the paperwork I've already allocated for that day. I find this very helpful at reducing my stress levels.

(Geography lecturer)

I buy myself extremely nice stationery for things it is important not to lose, such as an assessment record book. I have three different group seminars which I call my red, blue and green groups. I like to keep stuff for each group in a red, blue or green folder.

(Politics tutor)

I keep all the practical assessments in two cardboard boxes in the lab. Students hand in to one box and I hand them back in another. It stops me taking work home.

(Chemistry lecturer)

I use two concertina files for organising essays. In the first, I put essays in alphabetical sections. When I've recorded a grade and highlighted a feedback sheet, I put the essay into sections according to marks A–F. This helps me check the overall distribution of marks and really helps when I need to spend several separate sessions assessing a whole batch. In the old days I had essays all over the dining room table.

(Social Sciences tutor)

Information technology

We have an attendance spreadsheet on our PC during the practicals so that we can record attendance and some assessments during the session so that everything is up to date for when the lab is run again for different groups the next day.

(Chemistry lecturer)

I make it a matter of pride to clear my in-box of email every day I am at work. I try to deal briefly with each item at a set time each morning and afternoon. If it's a quick matter, I deal with it immediately, if it's more complex I make a note in my diary of when I will deal with it and acknowledge this with a quick reply by email. It's not always possible of course but it gives me the feeling that I am controlling my workload, rather than it controlling me, which is what I felt before.

(Modern languages lecturer)

We make sure that our departmental secretary is the guardian for all hand-ins. He gives out a receipt or a request for extension slip and ensures that timings are kept to strictly. I just have to pick up the full batch and get on with it.

(Arts lecturer)

I require students to submit a section of their final project electronically, before I give them the go-ahead to submit. I comment online and email a standard checklist where I point out ways they could improve. What I find is, this task is spread over a week or so and substantially reduces the amount of feedback and difficulty with the final project.

(Tutor of professional practice course)

I do find that the feedback which I need to give each time is substantially the same, so I can word process different versions of it and personalise it accordingly. However, my experience of discussing someone's work is always unique and can be very rewarding and creative in influencing their learning.

(Clinical Communications tutor)

PROBLEM SCENARIOS

 You find you are taking too long to complete the batch of marking. What can you do?

Make a realistic plan of the work in hand

Assuming you have not filled out a job assessment sheet do one now. For example, see Part 2. Can you justifiably reduce the amount of time you are spending per script by allocating your time to feedback common issues to the whole/part of the group, etc.?

Define your expectations

Define what you really mean by too long. Do you have unrealistic expectations of how quickly you can complete a major assessment? Are you doing this for the first or second time – it always takes longer until you are very experienced. Is it a new group? Have the students done very poorly?

Are you really hard-pressed because of other tasks, social engagements and commitments? In the short term you'll need to re-plan your commitments, perhaps cancelling or postponing those that can be put off. In the longer term, manage your optimism more carefully, always allocating lots of free time as a buffer zone round your planned time.

Compare your planned and actual times for tasks. Log your time to update your understanding of how your current time is being used. You may be skimping on time for rest and relaxation and so be tired and poor at concentrating and taking longer to complete work than at your best. Revise your expectations and take steps to put right the imbalance.

 You are midway through the term and you are finding it harder and harder to make progress with your research. All your time seems to be going on admin. What can you do?

Define your expectations

Define admin? Is this legitimate work which must occur at this point in the cycle and must be done by you? For example, registering new students, applying for a grant by a certain deadline, assessing first work, setting up projects. If so, re-adjust your expectations and prepare to make excellent use of your high quality time later in the cycle.

Note down what is dominating your workload this month. Predict what will still be there in three months, six months. The chances are the picture will look very different.

Review your practices

Is there something you are not yet doing efficiently? Are you doing repetitive jobs? Keep a note for a day of what you do: prioritise it. For example, label it A, meaning – my job depends on this, B – it's important to do this, and C – this would be nice to do. Note any system you'd like to improve – can you think of a way? Could you improve your paper/IT systems to help you?

Match your energy to the task. Keep your most productive time for your research work. For example, an hour of thinking every day first thing will encourage you to see the day as a success; your lesser amount of energy will be sufficient for completing more repetitive tasks.

You have left your notebook with half the assessment you have already done at work. You have only tonight to complete it. What can you do?

Oh dear. You are about to pay the price for rushing. Depending on your mood and personality you still have some options.

It is likely that you retain a good enough memory of what you have already assessed as far as standards go, in order to be able to continue assessing the remainder. You will need to put an extra stage in tomorrow moderating what you did in two stages and checking over the whole batch and ensuring that all obtain a similar form and amount of feedback.

You might want to get up very early and do the whole lot tomorrow. Your subconscious might be telling you to stop rushing and overworking and have an early night. Tasks done in the light of having made a mistake which we still feel angry about, when tired, can take much longer than when we are fresher and more optimistic.

FURTHER READING

Covey, S. (1990) *The Seven Habits of Highly Effective People*, New York: Simon & Schuster Adult Publishing Group.
Covey introduces interesting notions about managing priorities and quality of time as well as quantity. Although aimed at a US business audience, there are plenty of thought-provoking ideas about the work–life balance.

Johnson, L. (1996) *Being an Effective Academic*, Oxford: Oxford Centre for Staff Development.
Leslie Johnson has some sensible suggestions to make about organising the balance of your academic life which avoids the irrelevance of many business-oriented books.

Chapter 5

Issues in language and culture

INTRODUCTION

I wish to preface this chapter with a personal confession – I continue to be amazed at the poor standards of grammar and spelling which I repeatedly observe in handwritten work from . . . colleagues! I am also surprised to find that my own grasp of grammar and spelling loosens when I am writing on a whiteboard or flipchart in front of a group of learners. However, I observe an utterly professional and correct standard of written work in published and prepared documentation from the same writers. Clearly anxiety and context affect us all. No surprises then that our students struggle to provide written work of the standard we ideally wish for and identified in the Dearing Report (1997) as one of the chief communication skills which was vital for our students to develop in the future.

My aim in this chapter is to explore the strategies we can use to help students close the gap between imperfectly and incorrectly expressed work and achieving language facility, which will succeed even in pressurised situations such as written examinations. Assessing written work is a great opportunity to judge how our students' thinking and understanding are progressing and to help them find ways which will help them close the gap between their understanding and their ability to express that in a way that does them justice. For students working in languages other than their native tongue, this gap between the concepts they understand and the sophistication of language they use may be even more marked.

After many years of studying the products of writing we can help students develop their approach and enhance their processes of writing which will lead to much improved written work.

WRITING AS A PROCESS

In the USA there is an established tradition of working explicitly with the processes of writing; many colleges have been offering Master's and Doctorate level courses in writing for thirty more years than in the UK. A recent national resource which explores the links between thinking and writing and gives many examples from practitioners on how to tailor assessments to develop students' processes of writing is a web site developed at Queen Mary: the thinking-writing web site: <http://www.thinking-writing.qmul.ac.uk>. This resource is designed to help tutors question their current practice and see detailed examples of how other colleagues have extended the range of writing-intensive activities within their courses. The aim has been to raise the standard of written work students produce without increasing the amount of time assessors have to spend giving feedback. There are examples from across the disciplines; from modern languages and English to biological sciences (Figure 5.1).

Your role

You are a role model and authority to the students and therefore your use of language is important. In your spoken and written instructions for assessment it is a good discipline to ensure that the language you are using is not only free of spelling and grammatical errors but also avoids colloquial and proverbial expressions that can be impenetrable to those from cultures other than our own; make sure you are not excluding students.

Only you can define the extent to which you are prepared to spend time supporting students' difficulties at the boundaries of disciplinary knowledge. Many students are supported within the institution by a number of centralised services that are there to help you to focus your energies most productively. Students may have access to pastoral and academic support through a personal tutoring system; through providing generic study skills support appropriate to their level of study; through specialist support for special needs, such as dyslexia, dyspraxia, etc.

Many students may be tackling multiple challenges, for example, some international students may also be mature students, settling into a new physical and cultural environment and adapting to different academic expectations.

FIGURE 5.1
Writing in the Disciplines opening web page

Thinking Writing

A guide to writing-intensive teaching and learning

Sections :

- Getting Started
- Writing in Higher Education
- Effective Assessment Strategies
- Using Short Writing Tasks
- Developing Reflective Thinkers
- Frequently Asked Questions
- How We Can Help
- Join the Discussion
- Background at QMUL
- Subject Resource Bank

How to use:

Blue hexagons are the main thematic content sections. Work through these in order to gain a thorough practical understanding of the Thinking Writing approach. Red sections contain other useful information.

First time visitors should click on 'Getting Started', which explains more about the educational rationale of the site, and how to use it to suit your needs.

About:

This site is for Academic staff who teach in any discipline in UKHE.

It is designed to be:

○ A guide to using writing in your teaching
○ A practical resource
○ An introduction to a pedagogical approach
○ A discussion forum and point of contact

By:

The site is funded and promoted by the LTSN Generic Centre.

It was designed by Sam Brenton (Educational and Staff Development, QMUL), using text and materials from Sally Mitchell (Writing in the Disciplines project, QMUL), with project management from Catherine Haines (ESD, QMUL) and further guidance and contributions from Alan Evison (WID project, QMUL).

Copyright is retained by the authors and development team. Launched February 2003.

ltsn generic centre

Queen Mary University of London

ESD Educational and Staff Development
– Learning Development Unit –

Text-only homepage - Accessibility info- Home - Getting Started - Writing in HE - Effective Assessment Strategies - Using Short Writing Tasks - Developing Reflective Thinkers - FAQs - Background at QMUL - How We Can Help - Subject Resource Bank - Discussion

Your role is to ensure that you and your students have a clearer idea of mutual expectations and that you ensure that your time and attention are shared as equitably as possible among the needs of the group, fostering peer support as much as possible.

Many lecturers find that devoting extra input into feedback and expectations about language issues and processes of producing written work pay off handsomely later in the course. You must set and keep boundaries that you are able to maintain and divide the responsibility between you and the students.

Brush up your own language issues

We all have our own hazy areas of spelling and grammar. It may be worth investing some time in clarifying your own issues. Many international students will be much better than you at grammar; summarise your usual confusions and keep them handy when you write.

Put together a quick checklist of common confusions – agreements and homophones. For example, MS Word help offers suggestions for commonly confused words to consider. Encourage your students to use all the help available to them in their word processing software.

Technical language

Help students to build up a definitive glossary of the terms you consider essential and add examples in their own words from their own experience. See Chapter 3 for examples of terms and definitions and examples in assessment. Have a system to alert students to key words and concepts that they will need to define and use again. It may help to give extra credit in assessed work for correct use of technical language to show its importance.

A conversation I recently overhead in a university bookshop demonstrates how mysterious some students find our necessary terms:

Student one: Have you got an argument in your essay?
Student two: I think so . . . What is an argument again?

It is quite possible to use terms and even concepts without really understanding them. The more familiarly they are used, the less likely students are to confess their ignorance. Examples of vital terms which I find students commonly misunderstanding are: algorithm, paradigm, data, assessment, criteria, references and evidence. Make sure your students are clear what key terms pertain within your discipline.

SOME LANGUAGE ISSUES FOR SPEAKERS AND WRITERS OF LANGUAGE OTHER THAN ENGLISH

Recent figures quoted by the Higher Education Statistics Authority (HESA) indicate from their information on overseas students from HE institutions that the proportions of students who are likely to be studying other than in their first language is considerable: up to 10 per cent at undergraduate level, 25–35 per cent at postgraduate levels. For many subjects, institutions and geographical locations this is likely to vary. This is also true for teachers.

By definition, all students are successful learners. They have all evolved successful learning strategies which have brought them into your class. All your students may need to make and continue to make adjustments in order to flourish in new environments.

Setting your standards for assessing written work

As always, the best advice is to make your criteria as explicit as possible. Explain clearly to yourself, your fellow markers and your students exactly what standard is expected and rewarded:

> We are looking for publishable standard at this stage of work.
>
> (An Arts tutor working
> at Master's level)

> So long as students can show me they understand the concepts, I don't care if they write notes or bullet points, so long as I can read it and it answers the question – what more could I ask. I haven't written an essay since I was 15 either.
>
> (Science lecturer)

So, where do you stand on this continuum for your discipline, for your students, at their level of study and the context in which they are writing?

63

Prepared coursework

Students may need explicit guidance in selecting and using appropriate preparation and editing tools. For example, do you require all work to be work processed? What are your expectations for proofreading?

Incidentally, do you undertake to word process all of your comments in feedback to students in return? Could you use a commentary feature to achieve this on electronically submitted work?

Do you differentiate between style and structure and correctness? Do you penalise insufficient use of spell checking and word count tools? Do you focus on separate aspects of the writing process or always assess the whole?

Setting your boundaries

With summative work it is clearly an inappropriate use of your time to direct feedback to issues of expression. However, with most assessed work, your key role is to direct your formative feedback where it can make the most difference. Developing our powers of expression is a lifelong task, as many of you who are working on achieving publishable academic writing will appreciate from your own work. Only Mozart could write down the sublime first time.

HOW TO FOCUS STUDENTS ON THEIR WRITING

Encourage editing and proofreading

- 'Correct' the first and/or last paragraph fully, require the student to complete the rest.
- Penalise incorrect spelling and word count infractions heavily from the start.
- Require two versions of a piece of writing, pre- and post-editing, with students highlighting changes.
- Introduce and develop an editing/development checklist with students for use with all submitted, assessed work.
- Require students to use an editing checklist on a peer's essay and submit it; or respond to a peer's feedback and submit their re-written version.
- Give students some assessed credit for re-writing and re-submitting work.

Don't overwhelm students

- Comment only on one key aspect each time, for example, argument, introductions. Illustrate with a model and an 'avoid this' example. Be explicit about cultural expectations which affect this.
- Get the students to do the referencing for each other's piece of work.
- Set assessed tasks based on essay plans or introduction and notes and references only to encourage focus.
- Have students do some writing in class time. For example, set an essay question in the closing ten minutes of a lecture or seminar and get students to make bullet point notes of how they might answer it. Show them a model of the notes as a summary of the lecture.

Help them be familiar with the criteria

- Students assess sample essays, written answers or reports using material provided.
- Students submit their own estimate of the strengths and weaknesses of their own sections of work.
- Students précis published pieces of academic writing in your subject.
- Students review published pieces of work.
- Students re-write sections of published work in their own words.
- Students identify the structure and argument and evidence in existing pieces of work.

Provide feedback on the most helpful information

In all cases the guidelines for effective feedback apply. Strive for students to receive specific ideas of how their efforts succeed or not with relation to your criteria. Keep it simple, specific and behaviourally and action oriented. The students should end up with clear ideas of exactly what to do differently next time to improve their work and what they have done well and should keep doing. They need to have this information in time for it to influence their future development.

Consider the following examples.

Good. Confident work

Or

You clearly state your argument in paragraph one and use a strong range of sources to support it throughout.

You need to be more theoretically informed.

Or

Your essay would be strengthened by showing you are familiar (by referencing) the key figures in the field. At a minimum, Newble and Cannon (1991), Habeshaw (1994), Biggs (2000).

Try to direct all your comments away from personal comments about the student and directly towards 'behaviours' or actions which you want them to change in their work. It can be helpful to address common concerns to the group using the third person, for example, 'Students don't provide enough evidence'.

Criticism, particularly when coupled with a low grade, can be an emotionally charged experience for the student. Where they lack self-esteem, they may easily transfer your well-meaning advice about their piece of work to a global judgement of the failure of their whole self. There may also be cultural differences involved. For example, a US student may be used to considering themselves a Grade A student and may need reassuring that 60 per cent is a comparable point on the scale within the UK system.

Here's an example from feedback to a literature student:

75 per cent = *Clearly first class (forget about the arithmetically missing 25 per cent)*

(Academic, French literature)

For further discussion of issues in giving feedback to students see Chapter 2.

CULTURAL ISSUES IN ARGUMENT CONSTRUCTION

It is worth noting that cultural issues do not apply solely to issues of expression. Cultural traditions also apply to methods of constructing and presenting argument. In *A Guide to Teaching International Students*, Ryan (2000) quotes Hofstede (1991), 'Culture is learned, not inherited. It derives from one's social environment, not from one's genes.' Certainly, the changes we might be interested in fostering and our power to do so lie within our environment. Hofstede goes on to describe a tradition of presenting the argument that varies according to cultural environment.

The Western model is based on the Aristotelian model of 'questioning the questioner'. We might cite older references, or sages, in order to question their arguments; let's call it 'sages versus upstarts'. Other cultures may fundamentally differ and espouse an approach we may characterise as 'follow the master'. In another tradition a linear approach re-stating facts known already to the assessor may be seen as disrespectful, patronising and absurd!

When considering plagiarism, Carroll (2002) quotes an approach to presenting an argument often found in African and Asian students' work where a circuitous, discursive path may lead to the key points of the writing much later than we are used to. Criticism may also be inferred rather than definitely stated. We have only to consider the typically modest British approach to talking about one's achievements in comparison with an approach more common in the USA to see how emotional responses to difference can lead us to make strong responses in our judgements. This is a key point to note when we are assessing. To ensure fairness, validity and reliability we need to try to remove any unfair barriers and test what is really important.

Cultural issues in project work

Some students find project and other open-ended work among the least comfortable of assessment tasks in our repertoire. Some also struggle with work which centres on reflection on the personal response, such as portfolios and other reflective assessment tools. The same students may be used to excelling in methods British students find very stressful, such as extended memorisation and oral examinations. It is important to bear these factors in mind when designing, supporting and assessing written work, particularly in these open-ended areas.

SUMMARY

International students often share problems and characteristics with other groups which make high demands on educators, for example, mature students who may be returning to study as Access and Foundation degree students, or students relocating, establishing new social support systems, dealing with debt and financial issues, and adjusting to work at a new level. International students can be very highly motivated and have many skills from their old environment which will help them adapt to their new.

The first six months of a course are crucial for all students facing these challenges. The extent to which we can help students adapt and thrive in their new environment is key to our joint success. If you follow a constructivist school of thought, that all learning is built on what has gone before and integrates within existing learning, international students may face a greater challenge than most. If you can spell out the details of the environment they are adapting to, so much the better. Issues of learning are also tackled elsewhere in this series.

PROBLEM SCENARIOS

 A group of Chinese students collaborate well together on your engineering course. However, their mid-course assessment contains many similar language errors and shares the same lack of critical questioning of the authority in the field. What action do you take?

Repeat rules and reinforce student understanding

It is clearly time to reinforce the boundaries between cooperation, collaboration, and plagiarism, especially with respect to assessment. The whole group may benefit from an opportunity to review and ask questions about how this may to apply to their work on your course.

Foster climate of critical enquiry

Focus on the degree of challenge which you are expecting students to make towards the authorities in the field. Devote some class time to challenging an argument from an important source – or even your own argument! Brief all students on acceptable modes of challenging evidence and constructing arguments. Demonstrate this from your own work. Construct situations where students oppose each other's arguments and yours.

Vary the work groups

Unless you intervene, it is likely that students will continue to work in the same groupings. Try to encourage class work in different groupings ensuring that cultural mixes emerge and people have a chance to work with different cultures and approaches.

One of your tutees, new to the Nursing course, shows excellent comprehension and ability in discussion but their written work is well below your expectations. What do you do?

Help students to adapt to higher level study

Discuss with the student what they find challenging about writing processes, time management, editing, arguing. Break the process down and reward different steps in the process with assessment, especially formative feedback. For example, set tasks for students to produce essay plans which they won't need to write up, using bullet point notes to indicate the content. Perhaps focus on editing, getting students to re-draft a section of writing, their own or each other's.

Individual issues

If you suspect a student is struggling with fundamental language issues refer the student to specialist support, for example, in study skills, counselling, etc. Do not rush to diagnose and label a student as dyslexic, for example, without giving the student time to adjust and adapt and take on new ideas. Do not stigmatise support services in your approach. Where possible, encourage the individual student to seek support from their tutor.

Students complain of too much coursework eight weeks into the semester, yet you want to keep the momentum going and prepare them for the large assessed project you have set to complete their coursework. What could you do?

Adjust the coursework schedule

If you investigate and find the students' comments are justified, there are many approaches which would still allow you to develop student skills without overloading them. It is commonplace for all courses to require some written work at this stage and future evaluation will need to take account of this.

You could choose to scale down the final full writing task. You could also set some work which could be done and handed in during class so that students are not over-burdened outside class. For example, they could demonstrate their understanding of content through a comprehension test based on some text, by writing short answers to a range of questions, by submitting essay plans instead of essays, by completing Multiple Choice Questions or computer-based assessment. Help the students to concentrate their efforts and focus on where the marks are to be made.

> Students are struggling with the academic vocabulary in your subject. How can you help?

Highlight the vocabulary

Students may respond well to a systematic approach where you identify and define any term you use as you go along, however, they may need you to use assessment to get them to prioritise remembering and building this vocabulary for their own use. You could require them to compile a list of terms and definitions and examples on a regular basis and assess their completed list, or at least select a proportion at random to assess. You could require students to focus on this aspect of some academic publishing in your field, re-writing it for the lay person.

> Your students (many are international students) need to improve the way they present their arguments. They regularly request a lot of individual support from you, after lectures, outside of your office hours, etc. How best can you structure your efforts to help?

Argument as a theme for all

You may be able to use a short section of lecturing time to demonstrate how you wish students to approach arguments. You could develop this as a theme in your presentation of material. Students may not see the links between your input and their other classes. It might be worth asking colleagues who work with your students in other settings how they tackle this issue.

Extra support

You may be able to use some of your 'office hours' to offer extra group tutorials on a regular but planned and manageable basis. Seeing a small group is better use of your time than seeing students individually. You may be able to build a joint understanding between them which will allow you to withdraw from running the tutorial after an interval. Do not underestimate the power of your authority and individual attention.

 FURTHER READING

Bean, J. C. (1996) *Engaging Ideas: The Professor's Guide to Integrating Writing, Critical Thinking, and Active Learning in the Classroom*, San Franscisco: Jossey-Bass Publishers.

Coffin C. *et al.* (2003) *Teaching Academic Writing: A Toolkit for Academic Writing*, London: Routledge.

Cutts M. (1995) *The Plain English Guide*, Oxford: Oxford University Press.
An easy-to-read short book which describes, using many examples, how to write good, simple English.

 WEB SITES

A web site has been specially designed to show examples of how staff can use assessment to improve student writing in ways other than the traditional essay. There are examples from many disciplines:

http://www.thinkingwriting.qmul.ac.uk/

Here are some selected study skills sites which students may find valuable:

www.Howtolearn.com/personal.html

www.Fln.vcu.edu/intensive/avstyle.html

www.Scbe.on.ca/mit/mi.htm#ico

www.Snow.utoronto.ca/learn2/intwoll.html

Part 2

You and your assessment in the disciplines

Chapter 6

Assessing essays

INTRODUCTION

When we think of assessment we often assume that grading essays or completing exams are the primary tool. It is certainly a major means, however, there are many practitioners who suggest that we think more carefully about how we break down this skill and use assessment and feedback to encourage students to develop the complex set of skills and knowledge which the essay requires students to deploy.

Much has been written to challenge the tradition of setting the essay over and over again throughout a student's course. In a recent issue of *The Guardian* (10 June 2003), Richard Winter, Professor of Education at Anglia Polytechnic University, launches a challenge as follows:

> It's time we found an alternative to the student essay. For tutors across the country, it's marking time again and, reading essays, we realise that many of our students have yet again taken refuge in 'surface learning'. Failing to assimilate the significance of our courses into their understandings they produce instead what they think the tutor wants; a despairing and deceptive ritual, a superficial imitation of the outward form of learning rather than the real thing.

It is likely that the essay will play a major role in your assessment work and that you may be using essay titles which have been set by others, and the content addressed in lectures, even perhaps seminars, are outside your remit.

This chapter aims to help you to use your time effectively to encourage your students' learning through the grading and feedback you choose to give them. Assessing essays written under exam conditions is discussed separately in Chapter 10. Many of the comments of beginning teachers in Chapter 1 and the check-list for good assessment in Chapter 3, apply to assessing essays.

WHAT COUNTS AS AN ESSAY?

The essay is defined here as any planned piece of written coursework which is submitted for assessment. My definition includes short answer essays in sciences such as chemistry and biology, parts of the essay writing process, such as producing essay plans, literature searches, abstracts, reviews, reflective journals, portfolio commentaries and even long essays and dissertations.

In the associated chapter on projects, reports and dissertations (Chapter 7), extra factors which heavily influence the outcome of extended pieces of work are discussed, together with particular requirements outside the scholarly tone of academic writing, used in report-writing, case studies and case histories, court advice, etc.

WHY DO WE GET STUDENTS TO WRITE ESSAYS?

The dictionary definition of an essay, a 'short composition', derives from the French *essai* a 'trial', from *essayer* 'to try out'. Essays contain a suggestion that the writer is trying out ideas. Sometimes it seems that only the best, most motivated students truly present their ideas in this 'reader-focused' form, many are still trying out their ideas for themselves in a writer-centred way by the time the hand-in deadline arrives.

However, an essay is what we often assume when we talk about written work, particularly for arts, humanities and social science subjects. Because of its facility in providing written, accessible evidence of a student's current thinking, scientific disciplines are increasingly incorporating short answer questions in their assessment process. One reason we get students to write essays is because our discipline has always done so. Increasingly we can use alternatives and diversified writing tasks to develop the same skills, an issue explored in the thinking-writing web site referenced in Chapter 5.

It is worth stating that our students may not share the same understanding of what we mean by an essay, and may have little idea of what they are aiming for. It is unlikely that, even on an academic path, they will be required to write an essay after their time in FE and HE.

However, the skills and cognitive processes which they use to produce essays will be crucial to their ability to research, formulate and express the 'content' of the discipline.

The genre of the essay is, then, rather artificial. Students, particularly from other cultures and from outside the standard FE, HE and 'A' level route, may wonder why we require them to write in a formal way to tell us what they rightly expect us to know already. To criticise and dispute authoritative views may also be alien to them.

AN ANSWER IS ONLY AS GOOD AS THE QUESTION

This statement applies to many aspects of education but particularly to the essay. Many of us will have inherited essay questions or recall questions we have used in the past. Like a crossword puzzle, there are certain clues and triggers which can help you use this assessment tool more effectively if you share them with your student.

Bloom's taxonomy (adapted from Bloom, 1965) (Figure 6.1) can provide a helpful guide to the cognitive processing levels and responses which we are asking students to make. Essays are our main tool to get students to demonstrate this processing at the higher levels of the hierarchy and to incorporate the lower levels. In Chapter 2 we saw how our learning objectives and hence assessment objectives need to pinpoint the level and trigger the appropriate response (Table 6.1).

HELPING STUDENTS TO INTERPRET ESSAY TITLES EFFECTIVELY

Brown *et al.* (1997) describe some approaches inviting an essay response which share common characteristics.

Speculative

- How would Marx have explained the collapse of Eastern Europe?
- What would happen to the health of Britain if there were no more antibiotics available?

These questions invite the student to construct alternative realities encouraging them to provide a rationale for alternative views.

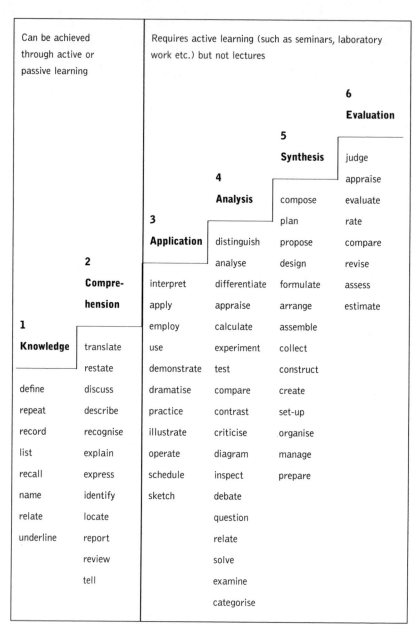

FIGURE 6.1 Bloom's taxonomy simplified

TABLE 6.1 Essay titles which relate to different levels

Summary	Key process word	Example title
Knowledge	Define, relate	Define three processes for producing lead commercially
Comprehension	Discuss, describe, identify	Discuss the key threats to the UK medical insurance industry market
Application	Interpret, illustrate, demonstrate	Interpret Blake's use of industrial imagery in at least two poems
Analysis	Compare, contrast, debate, examine, distinguish	Compare the advances in public health policy pre- and post-Second World War
Synthesis	Formulate, design, propose	Propose a re-structuring programme for the following situation:
Evaluation	Compare, assess, judge	To what extent is current foreign policy in the Middle East successful?

Quotation

A quotation adds another dimension to the essay response. It may be an amusing way of introducing a contemporary view on an issue:

> 'The current Education Minister calls medieval historians decorative.'
> Discuss with reference to education policy in HE in the last ten years.

Here the identity of the speaker is important to the question and could be used to prompt disagreement or defence.

Beware of including a quotation which simply conveys your question in a vague or confusing way and is long or confusing. This may operate as a trick question for students who are not on the same wavelength as you culturally or academically – which means most of them. These are best avoided in exams.

Assertion

1. 'Animals should not be used for experiments'. Discuss.
2. 'Animals should not be used for experiments'. Discuss in relation to the use of animals in the Japanese pharmaceutical industry.

79

3 Discuss the use of animals in the Japanese pharmaceutical industry.

These questions encourage the student to examine the pros and cons. Weaker students tend to focus on evidence in favour of their own viewpoint. The second question specifies some of the parameters of the discussion and is likely to lead to you being able to predict and reward student responses more fairly as the products will have more in common. The third example hides the question within the assertion.

Write about . . .

- Write about bricks (this is a real example from an architecture first year exam).
- Write an essay on sex and the epidemiologist.
- Examine the distinctive aspects of serial murder.

Weaker students can sometimes be attracted to this type of question; however, it is probably only a good choice for the brilliant student. Students are required to develop their own framework for this type of question. You therefore have to base your assessment on the success of their ability to satisfy their own framework. Open-ended essays can have their uses for more able or advanced students who are building towards defining their own topics for extended research or dissertations. For assessing more basic levels of content and recall, they are likely to lead to tremendous challenges to you as a fair assessor.

Describe or explain

- Explain the use of ANOVA techniques in experimental design.
- Describe the characteristics of light curing acrylics.

In essays these types of questions usually invite the student to give an account of or explain the rationale behind something. They can be useful at the lower levels of Bloom's taxonomy and for exam questions where marks are clearly indicated.

Compare and contrast

- Compare and contrast qualitative and quantitative methods of evaluation.

■ What are the major differences between the views of society of
Durkheim and Weber?

Comparison and contrast may be requested directly or indirectly.
These do not request the student's own views, however, able students
often draw a conclusion which summarises their position on the
differences.

Discuss

■ Discuss the role of Bismarck in the formation of the German
state.
■ Discuss some of the processes which are initiated by forms of
physical disguise or transformation in any TWO of the texts you
have read.

This type of question assumes that the student will assume a critical
stance and involve the processes lower down Bloom's hierarchy, descrip-
tion and explanation, comparison, and may also involve analysis and
evaluation from the higher levels.

Evaluate

■ Evaluate the impact of microcomputers on laboratory work in
undergraduate courses in physics.

Evaluation requires that the student is familiar with the evidence and
arguments but that is not the primary focus of the task.

Design

■ Design an experiment to test the hypothesis that redheads are
quick-tempered.
■ Draw up a specification of a recreational centre suitable for use
by people in the age range 55–75 years.

Sometimes this form of essay question requires quite detailed specifica-
tions and because it requires the student to apply their experience in
detail to a new situation, it can take longer to produce, and therefore
must be used with care in examination situations.

Problem-based essays

- You have been asked to give a talk on the ecological movement to the local conservative association. Prepare a draft of your talk and the answers to four questions that might be raised by the audience.
- What advice would you offer to a small textile company that has the following turnover and characteristics?

Witty questions

- Was 'The Excursion' by Wordsworth really necessary?

See the comments on quotation questions above!

ELEMENTS OF AN ESSAY

Checking the proposition in an essay

We and our students need to become adept at analysing and allocating effort and marks to the appropriate parts of the essay task. Table 6.2 shows a proposition checker adapted from Evison (2002) which encourages student facility with constructing their argument or responses.

Ideas and argument

In Chapter 2 on feedback we considered how feedback ideally needs to address the issues of idea and argument first, the higher order concerns. Different disciplines define the notion of an argument or thesis differently. However defined, the student is required to present coherent, linked evidence which they clearly set out, which addresses the question, which builds to a conclusion which satisfies the original intention and supports each step with accurate reference to a body of knowledge within the discipline. Clearly, this links closely with structure, which we consider next.

Students can be helped to recognise and gain feedback on these issues as an aid to constructing their own arguments. You might consider getting students to précis or construct abstracts of previously successful student essays (and each other's) in order to strengthen this skill. Students can debate positions, attack or supplement evidence, propose counter-

TABLE 6.2 A proposition checker

Steps	Example
Take an essay title	Should we modify animals genetically to produce organs for donations in humans? Discuss
Turn it into a statement – claim or assertion	We should genetically modify animals to produce organs for donation in humans
Express the opposing statement (defines the continuum of positions)	We should not genetically modify animals to produce organs for donation in humans
Add degree of qualification (defines positions on the continuum)	We should never genetically modify . . . Under certain circumstances, we should genetically modify animals to . . . Certain genetic modifications should be undertaken but others are unacceptable
Decide what kind of assertion this is: claim or controversy of fact	Is it or is it not the case? NO
Claim or controversy of definition	Do we all agree with definition of the phenomenon? NO However, the answer may need to address what we mean by genetic modification of animals.
Claim of value	Do we need to establish the quality, worth or morality of something? YES
Claim of action or policy	Do we need to establish a course of action? YES

arguments to their own or major issues and vote on the winners to improve their skill.

In your discipline it is worth considering what evidence in support of arguments is most impressive: a quote from the literature, factual evidence, comment from a literary text, historical evidence, census data, etc. Your assessment can identify and praise where students have been able to incorporate these arguments and advise where they could have done more or included something crucial. Students need to know how strongly this will be rewarded in their assessment.

Structure

It can be very useful to separate the structure of an essay from the content for the purposes of helping students select and employ the most

TABLE 6.3 Five common structures for presenting topics

Type	Description	Advantages	Disadvantages
The classical	The discussion is divided into broad areas and then subdivided	Easy, familiar, user defines topics	Potentially boring
Problem centred	Problem outline and solutions offered	Excites curiosity and interest	Favours third solution, simplistic conclusions
Comparative	Two or more perspectives, methods, models or eras compared	Flexible, allows for complex information	Must describe ideas before comparing
Sequential	Chain of reasoning for idea leading to solution or discovery	Exciting way of relating discovery	Easy to lose audience, chronology seldom best structure
Thesis	Assertion made proved or disproved through argument, evidence and speculation	Interesting	Can be difficult to follow – summarise and strong structure required

suitable. George Brown (Brown *et al.* 1997) has identified common structures which tend to match patterns of argument and needs of certain disciplines (Table 6.3).

Figure 6.2 shows worked examples using these structures for the proposition: Is it better for me to live in the countryside rather than the city?

If you can focus your assessment and feedback on the extent to which an essay adheres to a suitable structure beyond the beginning, middle and end, or employs an effective mixture of the above styles, this can help students progress and speed your feedback by referring to a common understanding.

Structure lends itself to being envisaged as a picture. Students could be encouraged to expand their skills by depicting the structure of their essays using outlining (offered in MS Word), spider diagrams, writing topics on sticky notes and moving them around until satisfied, or by submitting an essay plan which gives the first and last sentence of each section to show the argument and structure.

Classical structure

Introduction   A dilemma faced by many of us is whether to live in the country or the city.

Main idea 1   Health: •less pollution •more exercise likely •but more stress due to financial burden

Main idea 2   Finance: •higher petrol costs •property more expensive •insurance cheaper

Main idea 3   Quality of life: •slower pace •sense of community •fewer amenities

Conclusion   I don't mind the money. I'm moving to the countryside as soon as possible.

Problem-centred structure

Introductory statement of problem   Did you know, shocking fact

Possible solution 1   Make cities better places: •ban cars and cut pollution . . . (but) •make cities safer, reduce crime . . . but •encourage sense of community

Possible solution 2   Move to another country: •choose country where cities are cleaner . . . but •safer and friendlier . . . but •with low cost of living . . . but

Possible solution 3   Move to the countryside: •healthier •safer •quality of life

Conclusion   I don't mind the money. I'm moving to the countryside as soon as possible.

Sequential structure

Introduction   A dilemma faced by many of us is whether to live in the . . .:
   •Arguably healthier to live in the countryside because
       •Three reasons . . .
   Living a healthy lifestyle leads to: Less stress:
       •Three reasons . . .
   Leading a less stressful lifestyle leads to: Better quality of life
       •Three reasons . . .
   Better quality of life leads us to the conclusion that:

Conclusion   I'm moving to the countryside as soon as possible.

Comparative structure

Introduction   A dilemma faced by many of us is whether to live in the . . .

Feature 1   Health: •Countryside is not as polluted – the city is polluted •Countryside encourages exercise – city encourages poor habits •Countryside can be stressful financially – city can be less stressful financially

Feature 2   Finance: •higher petrol costs – city less petrol •property more expensive – property less expensive •insurance cheaper – expensive insurance

Feature 3   Quality of life: •slower pace – faster pace •sense of community – less community •fewer amenities – plenty of amenities

Conclusion   I don't mind the money. I'm moving to the countryside as soon as possible.

Thesis structure

Introduction   Living in the countryside invariably means a higher standard of living

Feature 1   Are country dwellers more healthy? •Exercise •stress •pollution

Feature 2   Finance: •transport costs •property costs •insurance costs

Feature 3   Quality of life: •pace of life •sense of community •amenities

Conclusion   In certain circumstances, such as mine, living in the countryside can lead to a higher standard of living, taking quality of life into account. I'm moving to the countryside as soon as possible.

FIGURE 6.2 Examples of structures with countryside topic

Marina Warner, eminent writer and academic, described one of the marvels of the writing process as follows:

> There is little in life where you can change your whole structure at the last minute. If you are an architect you can't be finishing off a building and suddenly decide that the cellar actually belongs in the attic. With writing you can.

People often work differently, of course. In an article on developing student writing skills, Louis Menand (2000) puts the opposing view: 'Would you tell a builder to get the skyscraper up anyway he or she could, and then to go back and start working on the foundation? I think not.'

Students often stick to the first structure that seems to allow them to formulate something in time for the deadline, with an increase in their understanding of structure and evidence, and with word processing they can substantially improve the coherence of their work.

Linking phrases

They may also benefit from collecting examples of how to link together their arguments into the structure and signposting the way. Students can build a stock of suitable phrases and strengthen the mechanics needed for producing an essay which flows.

Examples of linking phrases:

- One of the most striking examples
- Before discussing X
- Having considered arguments against
- In addition,
- While
- The problem can be summarised as follows:
- Similar themes emerge in the work of

FOCUSING ASSESSMENT ON THE DIFFERENT STAGES OF ESSAY WRITING

This next section is taken from the Coventry University materials produced to help students with their study skills.

IMPORTANT STAGES IN WRITING AN ESSAY

Everyone goes about writing essays in different ways. These notes are not an infallible recipe; they are just some ideas to help you. There are four main stages involved in developing an essay. They are:

1 Researching the content.
2 Reading the material.
3 Making an essay plan.
4 Writing the essay.

There are eight factors that can be found in any very good essay. They are:

- appropriate style
- good presentation
- arguments or ideas that are supported by evidence
- evidence of wide reading and an understanding of the subject
- clarity of thought
- originality of thought
- clear structure
- answering the question.

Essay marking criteria, Figure 6.3
This sheet tells you the sort of criteria staff agreed to use when marking essays on one module in 1993. There are many more in existence. It will be helpful to obtain the relevant criteria for your course or modules.

IN THE DISCIPLINES

Dr X did his essay marking more quickly than anybody else in the department so I asked him to show me how he did it. He read through and marked any part of the essay he wished to feedback about with a number as he went through. At the end he wrote a comment for each number. I took it one stage further and word processed the common comments onto a sheet and used the numbers to refer to the comments I'd already written up. It helped a lot.

(Humanities tutor)

87

Knowledge			
Text	Deep, thorough, detailed knowledge	☐ ☐ ☐ ☐ ☐	Superficial knowledge
Author	Wide knowledge used in analysis	☐ ☐ ☐ ☐ ☐	Knowledge lacking or not used
Genre	Wide knowledge used in analysis	☐ ☐ ☐ ☐ ☐	Knowledge lacking or not used
Historical and social context	Wide knowledge used in analysis	☐ ☐ ☐ ☐ ☐	Knowledge lacking or not used
Essay			
Structure	Clear logical structure	☐ ☐ ☐ ☐ ☐	Confused list
Quotations	Correct, purposeful use, properly referenced	☐ ☐ ☐ ☐ ☐	References lacking, or incorrect
Other sources	Wide range, relevant, properly referenced	☐ ☐ ☐ ☐ ☐	None or irrelevant
Grammar and spelling	Correct	☐ ☐ ☐ ☐ ☐	Many errors
Personal			
Response to text	Vivid, personal	☐ ☐ ☐ ☐ ☐	No response
Viewpoint	Clearly expressed	☐ ☐ ☐ ☐ ☐	Viewpoint lacking or unoriginal
Creativity	Imaginative, surprising	☐ ☐ ☐ ☐ ☐	Predictable
Critical theory			
Understanding	Clear grasp	☐ ☐ ☐ ☐ ☐	No grasp
Use of methods	Wide range, appropriately used	☐ ☐ ☐ ☐ ☐	Range limited

FIGURE 6.3 A sample feedback sheet for essays

I always write out the key concepts and terminology which I expect to see in each short answer before I begin and allocate marks to each. When I assess I just tick the script whenever I see them present and tot up the marks. If they are missing, I write them at the side.

(Biological Sciences tutor)

There cannot be a more concrete experience than confronting a stack of student essays ... What did I believe was important in making a fair assessment of student work? I decided there were three aspects of marking which often occurred simultaneously. One was considering the student's essay in the sense of what they had written on the page. Another was considering comments to make in response to what students had written. The third was to assign a grade to what had been written. It was this third aspect which gave me most concern.

(Graduate Teaching assistant in English Literature)

MARKS CRITERIA USED IN A DEPARTMENT OF ENGLISH AND DRAMA

A [70–100] signifies outstanding work. To earn an A, a piece must be independent, searching and detailed in its handling of material; it must be of the correct length, well expressed and well presented. Scholarly accuracy, originality of approach or argument, detailed investigation and evidence of wider knowledge will inform such an essay. Fluent and clear expression must enhance an argument which is original, stimulating and develops the topic relevantly. Mastery of the medium of expression – whether essay, project or studio or visual production – is essential. Needless to say, documentation should be impeccable.

B [60–70] signifies a substantial and interesting piece of work of the correct length, well expressed and well presented. To earn a B, a piece of work is expected to show careful study, independent thought, good organisation and fluent, accurate expression. It will make detailed use of primary and secondary source material, correctly documented, show critical enquiring thought, and make an articulate and informative, clear and relevant argument. This is a high mark and requires a piece of work which is not only sound but engages intellectually and productively with material and with the task assigned. A thoughtful response to complex issues or difficult material will often be the basis for such a mark.

C [50–60] indicates a sound piece of work of the correct length and satisfactorily presented. If the material could be handled in greater depth or detail this will be pointed out and exemplified. If problems of expression or presentation hinder the clarity or effectiveness of the argument, these will be noted. An argument must be developed which is organised and coherent in itself and responds relevantly to the topic. Points made in the argument must be backed up or illustrated by examples or evidence from the texts discussed. Sources must be properly acknowledged. The piece of work must handle the material competently.

D [40–50] indicates weakness in the standard of work. If the weakness is in the way the subject is addressed or handled critically the course leader will explain the deficiency. If it is in presentation clear guidelines or corrections will be offered. If the piece of work is too slight the student's attention will be drawn to the suggested word limit and suggestions made as to what else might have been included; if it is much too long the word limit will be noted and ways of cultivating economy suggested. If spelling is at fault, the proper instruments of old or new technology will be recommended. Other deficiencies in writing skills will be explained by advisers and/or course leaders.

F indicates an unsatisfactory piece of work. Work not handed in or work not the student's own automatically fails (also for the latter penalties are severe). An F may be given for a piece of work far too slight, far too careless in presentation or expression or completely failing to address the assigned topic or task. It would never be given for an earnest attempt to perform the exercise as directed. For a very unsound performance with acceptable presentation or acceptable content with poor presentation, an E might be given.

PROBLEM SCENARIOS

You've been given 80 essays to mark in two days for a new group. You want to give them good quality feedback to make your job easier in the future. What can you do?

Use a job assessment sheet to plan your time

Estimate a realistic amount of time per essay, plan for regular breaks to stave off tiredness and boredom. Allow time before and after sessions to moderate your own marking as a whole. Figure 6.4 shows a job assessment sheet.

Use a sampling method

Briefly scan a selection of essays, or perhaps the conclusion of each essay to help you judge the distribution of results against the criteria you have set. Check that the distribution of marks seems reasonable.

Provide feedback on common mistakes once

Produce a sample 'good essay response' which illustrates the main feedback to the group. Identify common mistakes that groups are making and address your feedback to these issues instead of repeating comments individually. Produce a simple set of criteria for this piece of work, use it as a tick list to indicate the strengths and development points to students. Indicate an individual's strengths as well as weaknesses.

You have given a lot of help and support to one student on his long essay. Your other student struggled substantially alone. How do you take account of this when you grade their work?

Experienced assessors will have in mind very clear boundaries when they are supporting students working on substantial pieces of work. They can then ensure they do not become over-involved and offer more support and impact on the final result than they feel fair. It helps to set out expectations clearly from the start. The issue of independent

Assessment	Essay Q'S
Content	Twentieth-century economic theory, concepts and data.
Essay style	Standard essay expression required, referencing sources.
Previous experience	Second set of essays from this group. First attempt poor language, ok content, poor arguments & replace – ask – module leader – normal at this stage. A few may fail the assessment at this stage, few good.
Anticipate problems	Expect they will find Keynes tricky and use insufficient referencing – prepare front feedback sheet.
Who & stage	First year's economics– 40% ESOL.
How many	38 [check policy – 1 late – 1 ill]
How much	2–3000 words i.e. 8–12 sides, average 12 pages x 40 + 400 pages 1 minute per page
Time per essay	10–12 minutes
Criteria/mark scheme	Adapted from dept general essay scheme + 50% content. PASS – to 2nd year – not degree.
Formative	Important opportunity to focus on argument and referencing, refer students to language help.
Summative	Grades reported to module convenor – 7 days – by email. A–F department standard scheme
Plan for feedback	10 mins with group at start of next seminar, joint start on general essay sheet + joint comments + individual + comment by student.
Plan to check standards	
Sampling	Read first and last page of 10 essays first – give grade. Brief table of distribution of grades:
Any additions	
Assessment plan	
Preparation	Put in alphabetical order. Dept mark scheme, mark book, feed back sheets.
Initial sampling	Assess 10 essays, initial grades given, put into piles.
Session 1	Assess 12 essays – 100 mins, feedback sheets, enter provisional grades. Add to notes – break.
Session 2	Assess 12 essays – 60 mins. Add to notes
Session 3	Assess 14 essays. Re-grade same sample at end – make any adjustments.
Record grades, submit, make copy, handover	
Remember for next time	
Issues to report to assessment organiser	
Issues to report to students	
Any other comments	

FIGURE 6.4 Job assessment sheet: worked example for essays

grading can be tracked by separating the formative and summative feedback role, enabling the summative assessor freedom to apply standards.

Students who under-use potential support, especially early on, may suddenly demand extra support near the deadline, which can be inconvenient and unfair on you. Again, set out expectations early; follow up and inform a student's tutor if students are not beginning the task. Make sure you and the students are very clear about what they are entitled to and perhaps get them to sign a learning contract to show they agree to the terms.

If you have no alternative but to grade, be sure to use clear criteria and apply them carefully to ensure you can justify your grading position. It might be worth consulting a colleague to find out how they deal with this issue and to ensure that future guidelines and criteria take account of this common problem.

 Some of the essays you have to assess are very mixed, containing excellent content or style, but substantially lacking in important respects. How do you grade them?

Criteria are your best ally here. It helps enormously if entries address common weak area such as style, language, referencing, content. If criteria have been used throughout, this should not surprise the students. Consult your colleagues if you believe a particular lapse is so serious as to merit extra penalty, or additional performance merit extra credit, for example, for originality. This problem is known as compensation. An effective criteria scheme needs to have some flexibility for you to exercise academic judgement in these cases.

 Some of your best students work together in and outside class. On the whole, you believe this has a good impact on their work. However, in their latest coursework they are expressing very similar ideas. How do you grade them?

Academics take different approaches to this depending on the circumstances and how they define plagiarism within their course. This situation might suggest that you re-assert your expectation and the importance of individuality or originality in work. This will depend very much on the discipline, literary criticism perhaps demands more originality than more scientifically focused work.

Your criteria should help you to penalise this aspect of the work effectively. In the worst cases you could reduce this 'score' for the appropriate section to ensure the behaviour you want. All students (and we ourselves) are strategic learners and respond strongly to assessment. Be prepared to justify your decision and chat with a colleague if you feel unsure.

 You have been given essay titles to set and assess which you think are vague and ambiguous. How much help can you give to your students and still be fair?

Personally, I think it is fair to ensure that students are not forced to guess what we want them to do. Introduce a list of essay key words, use Bloom's taxonomy or some framework consistently with them to help them interpret or choose what sort of essay answer they wish to make. Use some of the ideas above to support work on structure and argument.

FURTHER READING

Use the LTSN (Learning and Teaching Subject Network) for suggestions within your discipline. For an example from Philosophy:

Gough, M. *In at the Deep End of Essay Marking*, February 2001
      Accessed: 23 June 2003, from: http://www.prs-ltsn.leeds.ac.uk/
      philosophy/articles/gough/gough1.html

The following web site offers a brief discussion of how to support the development of argumentation, in the context of linguistics, but straightforwardly explained and perhaps useful across the disciplines:
      Accessed: 23 June 2003, from: http://www.lang.ltsn.ac.uk/resources/
      goodpractice.aspx?resourceid=1380

Chapter 7

Assessing reports and projects

INTRODUCTION

In this chapter we will be considering some of the issues which influence assessment for the student who is carrying out more individual work on a project, sometimes over a longer time. We will also consider some of the issues which affect the assessment of students giving accounts of their work to differing audiences through reports.

KEY ISSUES IN ASSESSMENT OF REPORTS, PROJECTS AND DISSERTATIONS

■ The majority of the lecturer effort is concentrated at the beginning and the end of larger, sustained pieces of work.

■ Helping students to choose appropriate projects and dissertations to study will help you to assess them fairly.

■ Motivating students is crucial to aid timely completion.

■ Addressing the emotional issues of a sustained piece of work is important.

■ Reports often have a pre-set structure but students require help clarifying the tone, content and evidence required for different audiences.

■ Formative assessment raises completion rates and standards.

■ Spread the summative assessment over several days and incorporate others in the process for fairness and reliability.

> ■ Reports, projects and dissertations are often linked with presentations and vivas (oral examinations) to tackle plagiarism and individual elements in group work.

Sustaining work over a period of time

The emotional experiences of producing a project or dissertation can be intense as the student is required to spend longer on a particular piece of work. This is reflected in the assessment weightings which are attached to project and dissertation work, often carried out in the final year of study and counting for a significant proportion of the final qualification result.

Lewis and Habeshaw(1997) quote a model from the Student Learning Centre at the University of Auckland which describes the emotional states common to students at each developmental stage shown in Table 7.1.

TABLE 7.1 Emotional stages of a sustained piece of work

Stage	Activity	Emotional state
First quarter	Selecting topic, establishing supervision	Excitement, giving way to boredom
Second quarter	Planning, reading and collecting data	Determination
Third quarter	Drafting and adding to data	Insight
Final quarter	Drafting, feedback, proofing	Despair, finally giving way to relief

Appropriate tone, language and evidence for the audience

A dissertation is usually subject to the same expectations for academic writing that have already been discussed, particularly in the chapters considering essays and language and cultural issues. But a project and a report are written for some purpose and often for a particular audience. For example, computer science students may be fulfilling a brief to recommend a new software solution for particular users, performance students may be reporting on performance work done in the community, engineers may be recommending a research solution to their peers or a practical process to improve a current situation. Students may well need help in identifying the needs of different audiences, particularly in the amount of specialist evidence or terminology which they can use to report on their findings. They may need to provide a glossary of unavoidable terminology or extend their writing skills beyond their existing writer-centred focus and address what the reader needs to know and therefore to do as a result of this project. This is a particular challenge for students working in languages other than their native language and for those without experience of the work environment.

Providing examples of successful projects, reports and dissertations

It is easier for a student to find their own examples of successful academic writing than of successful projects or reports because they tend to belong to the audience which commissioned them. It is a powerful way for assessors to raise standards and clarify understanding of assessment criteria to make successful examples available and invest time in helping students identify and assess for themselves the features of successful work:

> We didn't want students to be over-influenced by what others had done so we were reluctant to let students see past projects – after all, it is supposed to be creative and individual work. On balance, once the first lot had gone through, we thought it fairer to provide limited access to a variety of successful work, without the assessment attached and invite them to assess them themselves using the same feedback sheet we will use on them. My experience is that they are amazingly harsh critics of other people's work and this really helps them to clarify what they are aiming for. The creative ones will always find their own ways of doing things.
>
> (Business Studies lecturer)

Agreeing suitable projects and dissertations

As a project is a piece of work which has an end point, a one-off, there are many problems which assessors have to face to provide equivalent opportunities for students to succeed while still doing individual work. For example, can it have been done before? To what degree is the project open-ended or defined? How do students choose? To what degree do the marks depend on the success of the project in achieving its aims?

> These are genuinely open-ended research projects which allow MSc students to work with Research Assistants to produce real work. I provide some theoretically based projects too and advise students how to choose. There are the same risks as when students are choosing between exam questions, in my view, and the criteria take account of the process as well as the results, so it is possible to get a great mark with a project which technically has failed. We put a lot of effort into making sure students choose projects well.
>
> (Engineering lecturer)

> Students direct their own short theatre work and present the text and a variety of feedback from different sources. Of course they are all different, that's the point, but the resources potentially available from us are the same. How they use them is very different. They are required to report on the process and what they learned from the experience so sometimes they can get a much better grade if there's lots which went wrong, so long as they reflect well on that.
>
> (Drama tutor)

> We get first years to produce plans for their dream house on Hampstead Heath. They don't yet have deep technical understanding, but they can all relate to designing a dream house. This project has been done by countless students; many make the same mistakes but the results are always different. People don't change that much.
>
> (Architecture tutor)

LEARNING CONTRACTS

A learning contract is a document used to assist in the planning and execution of a learning project. It is a written agreement negotiated between the 'learner' and the 'teacher' that particular activity will be undertaken to achieve a specific learning goal or set of learning goals.

In the case of project supervision, commonly the student and the project supervisor will spend some time agreeing and drawing up a contract which spells out the roles and responsibilities of each side. It is meant to ascribe and agree roles of both parties and to ensure the smooth running of the projects. If problems arise, either party can have recourse to the written agreement.

Here is an example of a learning contract:

- The supervisor will make available an average of X minutes each week for supervision.
- If either student or supervisor cannot make a scheduled meeting, that person will give the other notice of this.
- The student and supervisor will agree a plan for the project work within the first two weeks of the semester.
- The supervisor will advise on matters of feasibility.
- The student is responsible for ensuring that the project conforms to all departmental guidelines on format, ethics, plagiarism, and style of referencing.
- The student is responsible for the literature survey.
- The supervisor will provide the student with written feedback on the draft of the project.
- The supervisor will not accept any drafts after the end of the Easter vacation.
- The student is responsible for accuracy of the final version of the project.
- The project is the student's property and s/he must hold final responsibility for it.

ISSUES FOR INDIVIDUAL ASSESSMENT AS CLASS SIZES GROW

There are a number of quick ideas which may help to streamline the assessment process. It may be possible to produce a list of common mistakes which you can highlight for individual students or provide a model answer and circle any points where a student has made an error.

You can limit the amount a student writes, encouraging them to be succinct and to the point, by structuring their report with specific questions or headings. The extreme version of this would be a series of key questions set as a multiple choice questionnaire which could be computer-marked.

It may be possible to sample assess, e.g. the student hands in all three reports, with a self-assessment sheet for each, and the tutor marks only two reports. Alternatively the student could select which two reports they would like to write up formally for assessment.

ISSUES IN PRODUCING JOINT PROJECTS AND REPORTS

It may also be possible for students to work together and build their team working skills through a project or report. The assessment process may need to be carefully structured so that the contributions of the individual are clearly assessed even though the project may have joint authors. Some assessors split the mark for joint work equally between participants, especially if it is at an early stage in a course. Some require the students to allocate a joint mark between them according to contribution, with statements justifying this. This process may need to be moderated by the tutor, especially the first time it is used. Other courses require individual reports on a joint project, sometimes backed up by a presentation or viva and questions where each member of a team may have to demonstrate their understanding. For more guidance on issues in group work, see Exley and Dennick (2004) in their book on group work in this series.

Structure

Reports and projects can be made easier for students and assessors by providing a framework structure. Reports are usually produced to meet a house style and to provide guidance for students is only simulating the business environment where reports are used:

> Students are required to produce a long essay on issues in medical ethics. It's part way between a report and a long essay. The focus is on their knowledge rather than their writing abilities and they are required to summarise the issues for an educated lay-person. I found it was impossible to assess 250 of these each year unless I became very prescriptive about the structure. I give them a set structure of headings which prescribes how they report on the legal basis and the ethical issues. If they follow my plan, they generally do OK and I can mark them much more easily against my model answers.
>
> (Lecturer in medical communication skills and medical ethics)

Study skills sites, such as at the University of Coventry (Cox, 1994), provide examples of suitable structures and a section of their materials for students on compiling a report is included here.

REPORT WRITING CHECKLIST

This checklist can help you to correct errors within each section of your report. Use it to help you when editing your reports or when you are asked to comment on someone else's. If you are considering your own report, put the first draft on one side for a day or two, then analyse it objectively.

1 Plan
- Is the plan of the report apparent?
- Are headings accurate and consistent with their purpose?
- Are the sub-headings the same throughout?

2 Introduction
- Does the Introduction state the subject neatly, and the purpose clearly?
- Have all the stated intentions been carried out?
- Is the title page complete and well laid out?
- Does the Introduction clearly state?:
  - the date of the investigation
  - who is submitting the report
  - for whom the report is written
  - the scope of the report
- Have you kept to your terms of reference, adequately fulfilled them, or exceeded them?

3 Summary – or Abstract, or Synopsis
- Is the report long enough to merit a summary?
- Is the summary too long?
- Is it objective?
- Is it relevant?
- Is it an accurate reflection of your purpose and your conclusions?

4 Facts – or Findings, or Results
- Could anyone accidentally or wantonly misinterpret any of your statements of fact?
- Are any facts mis-stated or exaggerated, suppressed or omitted?

- Have you omitted any facts or linkage between facts?
- Have you distinguished clearly between fact and opinion?
- Are there any apparent contradictions or inconstancies?
- Are the sources of the facts clear?
- Are your calculations accurate, and have they been accurately typed in the report?
- Are there vague descriptions where accurate figures could be used?

5 Conclusions

- Do the conclusions follow logically from the facts and their interpretation?
- Are there conclusions which are unwarranted by the evidence?
- Are possible solutions abandoned without reason?
- Do the conclusions remain objective, uncoloured by personal preference?
- Does the report contain all the necessary facts to substantiate your conclusions?

6 Recommendations

- If I were opposed to the recommendations, are there any parts in which I could pick holes?
- Are the recommendations practical and constructive?
- Are the recommendations within your terms of reference?
- Do the recommendations make clear what decision(s) if any are to be made and by whom?

IN THE DISCIPLINES

The London School of Hygiene and Tropical Medicine grade their project work at Master's level as follows:

Grading of in-course assessment employs an alphabetical four pass bands and two fail bands system using criteria appropriate for the task:

A	outstanding achievement, distinction level
B+	very good pass
B	good pass

C   satisfactory pass
D   borderline fail
E   outright fail or not submitted.

It is important that criteria reflect an appropriate standard so that bias in outcome related to choice of Unit, rather than the achievement of the student, is reduced. Further, it is anticipated that group assessment tasks should produce higher standards than individuals would achieve alone.

 ## Tips from experienced assessors of projects, reports and dissertations

In order to help students see that a report only has meaning for the people it is reporting to, I get my second year business students to present their findings first of all. They work in a group and are assessed on their ability to present their findings to an audience. Individually, they then write up their own report, incorporating feedback based on the questions their audience have for them. I give members of the audience roles for them to base their comments and questions on to incorporate different viewpoints. I find this sharpens their ability to structure and express their findings appropriately.

(Business studies tutor)

I get students to submit the executive summary and an outline of three reports they could make, presenting software solutions to users, but I only require them to fully write up one for full assessment purposes.

(Computer software development tutor)

I find students either respond to a lengthy project by becoming a shirker or obsessed with it to the point of damaging their other studies. I try to make it really clear in supervision sessions, which category I think the student is in and make sure they know it represents 25 per cent of their final year mark, one sixth of their degree, but that their other studies need to fit round it too. I use a written contract to spell out what the responsibilities of the student are and what exactly the responsibilities of the tutor will be. This helps me to show that I have given 'adequate supervision' in the event of a disputed grade.

(Electronic Engineering tutor)

103

I like to offer open-ended genuine research questions to the Master's level students as the course is intended to develop their skills in practice. I involve my research assistants in providing regular weekly group supervision in the initial phase of the projects. This ensures that students are competing with each other so they can judge their progress and effort and have access to more detailed help early on that I could provide alone.

(Electronic Engineering tutor)

I set up action learning sets which meet each week for the two terms that the project runs. Students meet in groups of five or six and give an account of their progress to each other and seek feedback and help from others in the group. This is a creative writing project, students are required to produce part of a novel or a collection of poetry and that can be a lonely and subjective business. It really helps motivate them to know that other people care about their progress. It helps them to observe the process of creation as well as the product, both of which they are required to submit.

(Creative writing tutor)

I found students really struggled with deadlines so I introduced a false and very early deadline. The full 6,000-word-long essay is not required until Easter, however, I require them to submit a plan or a draft before Christmas. Those who submit a draft have the added incentive of extra tutor feedback.

(History tutor)

We manage the amount of tutor help which students get by giving them a ration of supervision time to which they are entitled. When that's gone, it's gone. Their budget includes more time if they book supervision in groups or if they can submit their questions by email which can then have the answers posted to the course web site to benefit all students.

(Computer Science lecturer)

The participants have to present a portfolio covering their development over two to three years of work-based, part-time study. They meet with a panel of assessors to viva their work. It's fairly informal and at the end we can usually assure candidates that their work is being recommended as a pass to the Exam Board. It provides a positive way of completing this sustained piece of work and reduces the impact of the inevitable gap between handing-in and formally confirming the result.

(Professional Practice tutor)

Assessment	Final year demographics projects
Content	Level 3, some Master's level responses; some original data/primary sources, competent evaluation, informed by multiple viewpoints.
Report style	Publishable standard, fully referenced, formal academic writing.
Previous experience	Read last year's projects, supervised own, co-assessed and compared with Dr Y. Students – inexperienced with large writing projects.
Anticipate problems	Supposed to assess those I didn't supervise – check. Expect problems with statistics, structuring a long piece of work, sloppy standards towards the end. I've got a lot on this week.
Who & stage	Final year, final term.
How many	15 projects
How much	6,000 word limit = 25–30 pages x 15 = 450 pages max 1 minute per page
Time per report	20 minutes
Criteria/mark scheme	Dept. degree classification, project feedback sheet.
Formative	Detailed feedback required.
Summative	Main purpose – degree classification.
Plan for feedback	Individual sheet and report, when grades ratified during final tutorial before exams.
Plan to check standards	Moderated by Dr X – get them to her by Friday.
Sampling	Re-assess one at borderline of each degree classification.
Any additions	
Assessment plan	
Preparation	30 minutes – take home in 2 batches, check stuff
Initial sampling	30 minutes – Read intro of 5, conclusions of 5, notes
Session 1	3 reports: 60 minutes – feedback tick sheets as go, + notebook for personal feedback for each. Mini break.
Session 2	5 reports: 60 minutes. Break 20 mins.
Session 3	5 reports: 60 minutes
Session 4	Final 2 reports: 30 minutes. Re-assess borderlines: 30 minutes Word process individual comments from notebook: 60 minutes

Record grades, submit, make copy, handover to Dr X.

■ **FIGURE 7.1** Job assessment sheet: worked example for projects

■ TABLE 7.2 Project marking guidelines – Year 3

Proposals	Working with supervisor
70–100 • Draft proposal, final proposal and ethics submission[1] all submitted on time • Final proposal in correct format, written in very good style; spelling and grammar checked • Background to study very well explained and well referenced • Methodology well designed, well argued and well referenced • Scope of project realistic and well defined • Plans for analysis detailed and appropriate to data • Possible outcomes suggested and interpretations given with reference back to the literature	• Student takes lead in arranging meetings with supervisor • Student takes lead in arranging suitable work schedule • Student contacts supervisor appropriately in case of difficulties or queries • Draft literature review and methodology chapters and plan for data collection/analysis[2] submitted as agreed with supervisor and of a high standard • Student shows a responsible and mature attitude in all aspects of work with supervisor
60–69 • Draft proposal, final proposal and ethics submission[1] all submitted on time • Final proposal in correct format, written in appropriate style; spelling and grammar checked • Background to study explained and referenced • Methodology appropriate, argued for and referenced • Scope of project realistic • Plans for analysis appropriate to data • Possible outcomes suggested and interpretations given	• Student takes lead in arranging meetings with supervisor • Supervisor may take lead in arranging suitable work schedule • Student submits work as agreed with supervisor • Student contacts supervisor appropriately in case of difficulties or queries • Draft literature review and methodology chapters and plan for data collection/analysis[2] submitted as agreed with supervisor and of a reasonable standard
50–59 • Draft proposal, final proposal and ethics submission[1] all submitted on time • Final proposal in correct format • Some background and references given, but may lack detail • Methodology appropriate, but may lack detail	• Student may need to be reminded of need for meetings • Supervisor suggests suitable work schedule • Student submits work as agreed with supervisor • Student usually contacts supervisor appropriately in case of difficulties or queries

TABLE 7.2 *(continued)*

Proposals	Working with supervisor
• Scope of project may be under-defined • Plans for analysis appropriate, but may lack detail • Possible outcomes suggested but not interpreted	• Draft literature review and methodology chapters and plan for data collection/analysis[2] submitted as agreed with supervisor

40–49

• Draft proposal, final proposal and ethics submission[1] all submitted on time • Final proposal may be in incorrect format • Brief background given, may lack references • Methodology brief but seems appropriate – not argued for or referenced • Scope of project may be over-ambitious or too narrow • Plans for analysis brief and difficult to evaluate • Suggested outcomes brief	• Student is occasionally late for or absent from meetings • Supervisor occasionally needs to remind student of work to be submitted • Student occasionally submits work late, or not in form agreed with supervisor • Student may delay contacting supervisor in case of difficulties or queries • Draft literature review and methodology chapters and plan for data collection/analysis[2] submitted late, or content insufficient

0–39

• Draft proposal, final proposal and/or ethics submission[1] submitted late • Final proposal in incorrect format, inappropriate style, spelling and grammar errors • Proposal lacks background information • Methodology inappropriate or impossible to evaluate • Scope of project entirely inappropriate • No plans for analysis given • No suggested outcomes given	• Student is repeatedly late for or absent from meetings • Supervisor repeatedly needs to remind student of work to be submitted • Student repeatedly fails to submit work on time or in correct form • Student does not contact supervisor in case of difficulties or queries • Draft literature review and methodology chapters and plan for data collection/analysis[2] not submitted, or of unacceptable standard

1 Where appropriate.
2 Or other work as agreed with supervisor.

■ TABLE 7.3 Dissertation marking guidelines

Project	Dissertation
70–100	
• Student took full responsibility for organising and managing project; prepared well for tutorials and worked independently, keeping to agreed schedules • Student drew well on previous modules and a thorough literature review to inform the design of the methodology, analysis and interpretations • Very good understanding of methodology and analyses used	• Creates a coherent whole, guiding the reader through to a well-reasoned conclusion • Appropriate and accurate referencing throughout shows broad reading and a thorough understanding of relevant facts and issues • Findings interpreted appropriately and realistically within the research context; alternative interpretations discussed cogently
60–69	
• Student showed a responsible attitude, generally managing the project well; prepared for tutorials and often worked independently, keeping to agreed schedules • Student used knowledge from previous modules[1] and a literature review to inform most stages of the project • Good understanding of methodology and analyses used	• Structure generally clear, sections linked together, and the reader can follow the line of argument • Generally appropriate, accurate referencing throughout shows a good range of reading and an understanding of relevant facts and issues • Findings interpreted appropriately; attempts made to relate them to the research context and to discuss alternatives
50–59	
• Student attempted to manage project but more reliant on supervisor's direction; did not always make full use of tutorials • Student may have needed guidance to use knowledge from previous modules and a literature review to inform the project design • Adequate understanding of methodology and analyses used	• Sections linked together in most places; attempts to guide reader to a reasoned conclusion • Adequate referencing in most sections; evidence of a range of reading and reasonable understanding of relevant facts and issues • Findings interpreted adequately; reference made to the research context
40–49	
• Student very reliant on supervisor at all stages of the project, or managed project poorly; may have had difficulty keeping to agreed schedules	• Links between sections sometimes unclear; reader has to work hard to follow the argument

TABLE 7.3 *(continued)*

Project	Dissertation
• Knowledge from previous modules and literature review inadequately used to inform project design • Poor understanding of methodology and analyses used	• Reading inadequate and/or poorly understood; weak grasp of relevant facts and issues • Findings interpreted inadequately; little attempt made to relate them to the research context
0–39 • Student over-reliant on supervisor or mostly absent from tutorials; failed to keep to schedules • Little attempt made to use knowledge from previous modules and literature review to inform project design • Little understanding of methodology and analyses used	• Little overall coherence; reader cannot follow the line of argument • Insufficient reading and little understanding of relevant facts and issues • Findings inappropriately or inaccurately interpreted; relationship to research context poorly understood

Source: University of Manchester, Human Communication and Deafness Group

Accurate presentation is important: up to 10 marks may be deducted for poor spelling and grammar.

Figure 7.2 (p. 105) shows an example of a job assessment sheet; Table 7.2 (pp. 106–7) shows an example of marking guidelines; and Table 7.3 (pp. 108–9) an example of marking projects and dissertations.

PROBLEM SCENARIOS

 You have agreed to supervise some projects next term in your specialist subject and to second mark them.

Issues in project source

Establish how the scope and scale of projects will be agreed on. Do you provide some suitable topics? Are some projects harder than others? Which will need more resources/support?

Issues in project choice

How does your department handle the amount of support given in its impact on grades? Some choose to reduce the available marks, for example by 5 per cent when a project is defined by the lecturer rather than the student. Students who require a lot of help in order to complete their project might have account taken of this in their mark, to enable assessment to be fairer for those who do most of the work themselves.

Set your standards

If you can, study some previous projects and the examiner's comments and get a co-assessor to establish which are examples of good, OK and failing level work.

Prepare to brief the students

If you will be briefing the students, can you establish the requirements with the other assessors beforehand? You could plan hand-outs and seek documentation which can help you and your students to have a joint understanding of the requirements, particularly the assessment requirements for resources, hand-in dates and milestones, submission details, etc.

It's a good idea to set some pre-assessment deadlines for the students and for you to agree a learning contract which spells out important dates, for example, the latest date they can change project, a date when they have to have submitted a plan, a first draft and the final version. Make sure you and the students spend time clarifying the criteria for assessment.

Save time where you can

Can you combine supervision times for several students at the same stage, particularly for the procedural briefing at the start when they all need a lot of attention quickly in order to get going? This could also encourage peer-working, perhaps sharing reading, editing, referencing tasks?

Plan how much time and when you will be able to allocate to students and still preserve your own valuable time. It is a cautious but useful task to design and make brief records which students can sign to prove that you have offered the necessary supervision to them at the crucial stages.

FURTHER READING

Cox, S. (1994) *Report Writing*, Coventry: Enterprise Capability Workshops, Coventry University.

Lester, J. D. (1998) *The Essential Guide to Writing Research Papers*, New York: Longman.
A useful reference text which gives examples of finding a topic and worthwhile sources, keeping track of them and expressing them without seeming too daunting.

Lewis, V. and Habeshaw, S. (1997) 53 *Interesting Ways to Supervise Student Projects, Dissertations and Theses*, Bristol: Technical and Educational Services Ltd.

Chapter 8

Assessing practicals and fieldwork

INTRODUCTION

This chapter examines some of the issues which may occur in assessing practical work in addition to the guidance on feedback, setting and defining criteria and managing time provided in earlier chapters. A great deal of the staff time in supporting practical learning is directed at supporting and filling gaps in student understanding of any documentation and giving formative feedback to enhance student learning.

LINKS BETWEEN PRACTICAL WORK AND ASSESSMENT

Whether you are a lecturer working with demonstrators to help you to assess practical work or a demonstrator, it is likely that there will be a tradition of spending a great deal of effort organising students' time in labs (or on trips, or in rehearsal) which is often not closely linked to the assessment process.

As assessment is one of the most powerful tools you have to drive attendance and student attention, most courses choose to allocate a proportion of the marks on a course accounting for practical work. Often the emphasis is on helping students develop a professional skill or attitude through repeatedly producing reports of all the practical work that they do. In order to ensure that they do this, someone in authority usually looks at them and allocates some feedback or even a grade. Arts and humanities-related disciplines such as geography, psychology, even drama may include a large proportion of practical work.

Other disciplines may require students to demonstrate satisfactory skill in some area. For example, teaching, dentistry, and medical subjects often require the student to reflect on the process and their learning, giving a written account as a major component of how that is assessed. For example, teacher training traditionally requires students to submit many lesson plans and evaluations. This and Chapter 9 on problem solving skills and extended pieces of work may all have some ideas to contribute to your work.

 KEY ISSUES IN ASSESSING PRACTICAL CLASSES, FIELDWORK AND PERFORMANCE

- You don't have to assess everything every time.

- Be clear about what you are assessing and give feedback on that.

- Direct most time where it really counts for most students.

- Lecturers, technical staff and demonstrators all have to work together to support the learning.

- Model answers and excellent documentation can make a great deal of difference to performance.

- With fewer resources and collaborative tasks, individual assessment can become blurred without careful consideration of plagiarism.

Provide a model

When students start, they may take a long time to grasp what they are aiming towards. If you can, arrange for students to be able to examine successfully kept accounts of laboratory and fieldwork from previous years. Arrange for them to use the same feedback sheets that will be used on them and to assess this work in order that they are clearer about what they are aiming for.

Help with structure

The traditional structure of introduction, methods, results, and discussion sounds straightforward, but, within that, students often struggle at a paragraph level. They are unclear what exactly does go into an introduction and what to discuss first. Perhaps students can initially be assessed for completing a gapped model report, inserting their results, drawing one or two conclusions in note form, before progressing to producing more of the report themselves as they gain in skill and confidence.

Students can allocate one section each to members of a team working together and hand the report in as a whole. This could encourage peer pressure to ensure that all the sections of the report relate to each other and meet a minimum standard.

Help with writing

At a sentence level students often lack confidence and experience in producing polished written work. They can be unsure of the standards of expression, grammar and spelling necessary in such work. See Chapters 2 and 5 for more suggestions on giving feedback and encouraging students to write fluently and correctly.

It is customary in scientific writing to emphasise the objective nature of the enquiry by never mentioning the author or any subjective experience. In language this is often emphasised by adopting the passive mode of expression rather than the active. Unfortunately, passive expression can be extremely dull to read and understand, particularly over and over again as you assess scientific reports and writing. It is possible to express events objectively using the active tense. For example:

> The experiment shows that carbon can react with sulphide in the presence of oxygen.

Rather than

> It has been shown that . . .

Fortunately, Word and such packages provide a simple way of checking for the passive mode in your writing. Encourage students to use them.

A note on plagiarism

Repetitive tasks which cannot be changed radically from year to year are prime targets for copying and plagiarism. It can be helpful to define with students a clear understanding of where you consider the boundaries of plagiarism to lie for their work with you. Some lecturers get students to sign a statement confirming that they understand the differences between cooperation, collusion, plagiarism and cheating. Scientific enquiry has recently come under a lot of criticism for even eminent scientists being unable to prove that their work is entirely free from any hint of falsification. Students may be interested in any examples of this you may be able to give from your own discipline.

Some lecturers reinforce this strongly, early in the course:

> look for the smallest indication that students may have been copying their results early on. I immediately give a severe lecture to the whole group and deduct marks from the whole group to encourage peer pressure to control this – if some are copying, others must be involved. If I do this early in the first year, I usually have little trouble for the rest of the course as the students know I am serious about this.
>
> (Chemistry lecturer)

Encouraging students to complete part of the assessment during the class can also control this. For example, results can be handed in or checked by demonstrators before students can leave the class. You can require the students to complete a set of brief questions linking their experience of the work with the stated learning objectives to ensure they are making connections between what they are required to do and how it links with the material they are covering in the rest of the course. These techniques can help students to feel it is important to prepare for each practical, rather than wasting valuable lab and tutor time working out what they are supposed to be doing. You could encourage this by requiring them to show some evidence of their preparation at the start of the session, or have it available for spot checks during the session by you or demonstrators.

Students will still need to work cooperatively during practical work: there are insufficient resources and justification for everyone to complete tasks in parallel. However, you could require students to clearly distinguish between tasks they have to accomplish alone for assessment purposes, and tasks which they may share out between them. They could preface their reports with a brief statement about the role each of them undertook for example.

Encouraging problem solving and cognitive processes

Often students may be so concerned with managing the many different aspects of lab work – the equipment, the techniques, the results, each other, health and safety, etc. – that they may easily avoid thinking! If our assessment is to be successful in promoting scientific enquiry and problem-solving abilities, this must be specifically stated in the learning objectives for a session and preferably assessed. For example, instead of always reporting on what did happen, you can assess the students' ability to speculate using 'what if' thinking for experiments which they will never be expected to carry out.

We often save the motivating experience of carrying out a research project until the student has acquired two years of basic techniques, skills and knowledge. However, the principles of scientific enquiry, the excitement of investigating new processes (even if they are not new to you) can be incorporated from the start into assessment. This can be a motivating feature, both in the informal feedback you provide by questioning your students, challenging them and supporting them through their enquiry, and by explicitly requiring this through assessment.

Time and record management issues for practical classes

Lab and fieldwork is particularly demanding on your organising skills. You will be dealing with large numbers of students perhaps repeating the same classes on different days, coordinating the efforts of different groups of demonstrators, making sure equipment is well managed by your technical support staff, comparing notes with colleagues who may be running labs on different days. If you are involved in fieldwork, you may be away from all your normal office and organisation systems so that if you make a mistake and forget something, it can have serious implications on everybody else's work. It makes sense to double your normal preparations and make sure you have invested time and effort in setting up suitable systems before you start. Your colleagues may have already evolved systems which work for them and already used them with technical staff and demonstrators in the labs.

For example, some lecturers pay the demonstrators for an extra hour after the lab time in order to hold a 'marking party'. This is an enjoy-able sounding way of making sure that several people work together with model answers and joint feedback sheets to assess the lab work while it is still fresh. This has many advantages. No paperwork leaves the lab. Assessed work is simply put back in the slots in a box kept for this purpose, for the students to fetch when convenient for them or at the start of the next class. Assessors can ask each other questions which crop up at the time and compare notes to moderate their assessment. The lecturer gets immediate feedback about the students, the practical and the standard of assessment of the demonstrators.

Figure 8.1 shows an assessment sheet for practical reports.

Kate Exley, in her article in *The Times Higher Education Supplement*, 22 June 2001, summarised demonstrators' responsibilities as follows:

> Getting ideas on how to reduce marking time for conscientious demonstrators is important because many PhD students are expected to spend no more than six hours a week on teaching-related activities, as stipulated by the research councils.
>
> Suggesting that they could produce a summary page of feedback or commonly made mistakes which could be individually annotated and attached to the back of marked reports might help.
>
> Or, otherwise, a model answer or a worked example could be provided to show where improvements could be made. Using feedback forms or tick-box grading sheets to indicate where marks have been lost or gained can also provide a shorthand but effective ways of giving feedback to students.

 ## IN THE DISCIPLINES

What I didn't realise about the fieldwork trip was that we would be on duty for twelve hours a day, supervising students while they wanted to have a bit of fun. That meant that my conduct had to be super-professional and that I had to find some way to unwind even though my supervisor was there.

(Geography demonstrator)

I used to spend the whole lab session with a constant queue of students waiting to ask me questions. I was exhausted and I realised that any assessment was testing my performance! I took a step back and decided to divide up the room between the demonstrators and ration students to one golden question to me each per session. The students were fine about it, but if I hadn't changed my behaviour, it would have gone on forever.

(Chemistry lecturer)

Assessment	Lab reports titration CM101
Content	Gapped sections for results and methods, full introduction and discussion of strengths, limitations and applications of the technique.
Writing style	Full, correct objective scientific style required for introduction and discussion, results correctly given with full notation. Spelling and grammar penalties apply.
Previous experience	First year class, semester two. Familiarity with lab report structure and style assumed at a novice level. Recording of results expected to be accurately noted – previously focussed on in last assessment.
Anticipate problems	3 groups struggling during practical, one gained no usable results, substituted other group's results. Expect introductions poor and disorganised discussion from most.
Who & stage	1st year Monday group
How many	35 reports out of group of 40 first years [check attendance actions]
How much	5 pages per report limit x 35 = 175 pages – 1 minute per page + 2 checking
Time per report	7 minutes
Criteria/mark scheme	Use model answer (marks out of 60–10: results, 10 methods, 20 intro, 20 discussion).
Formative	First opportunity to see and comment on writing capabilities.
Summative	Contributes to pass mark required to progress to second year. To be entered onto departmental database for labs by Friday.
Plan for feedback	5 minutes at start of Monday lab; model introduction and discussion (written by demonstrator – check and correct and print it); invite them to re-write.
Plan to check standards	Compare grades with Wednesday's class (See Michelle), compare distribution within categories.
Sampling	Re-assess first, one from middle and last again.
Any additions	
Assessment plan	Preparation: 30 minutes
Initial sampling	Skim read 3: 10 mins
Session 1	Ten reports: 50 mins. Summarise notes (5 mins) check time – break, speed up
Session 2	25 reports: 100 mins. Summarise notes for feedback. Break
Sampling	sample 3
Record grades	Complete grades table

FIGURE 8.1 Practical reports assessment sheet

PROBLEM SCENARIOS

 Some of your students on the field trip are larking about when they should be sampling the flora. They usually still get adequate results in class. Is this a problem?

Health and safety concerns

The primary reason practical work is so expensive is because of the cost of providing a safe, well-equipped and supervised learning environment. It is important that you and the students are aware of their responsibilities for health and safety. However, if students are in a relatively low-risk environment, are completing the tasks adequately, their enjoyment may enhance their learning.

Gentle reinforcement of boundaries of behaviour

Approaching students and engaging them in conversation about their work will usually calm things down and help them to re-focus on their task. Some firm crowd control rules may be needed for large groups or potentially risky situations and these need to be kept simple, agreed with students and carried out if necessary. With firm ground rules, most of the time assessor attention will be enough to bring student behaviour back into line.

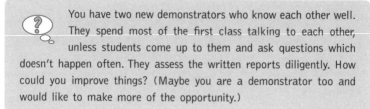 You have two new demonstrators who know each other well. They spend most of the first class talking to each other, unless students come up to them and ask questions which doesn't happen often. They assess the written reports diligently. How could you improve things? (Maybe you are a demonstrator too and would like to make more of the opportunity.)

Shy, inexperienced demonstrators

It seems your demonstrators do not yet understand their active role in giving formative feedback and assessment as well as summative (grading). Inexperienced demonstrators can tend to be shy and not aware of their potentially powerful role in assessment.

119

Divide up the room, allocate responsibility

Try allocating different sections of the teaching room to them and set them targets to interact with each student at least once during the session. Agree and suggest ways they can approach the students. Explain to the students what you are expecting. Encourage friendly competition between the demonstrators.

Arrange the room so there is an easy way for the demonstrators to approach students or groups and sit down at the students' level. They can wait for the students to ask them something or use neutral encouraging open-ended questions.

Useful questions and phrases for demonstrators are:

So, explain to me where you're up to.

This one's quite hard, isn't it?

I found this one tricky when I was preparing it

Do you want me to check anything with you?

Praise and reward your demonstrators when they do what you want. Demonstrators sometimes need to prompt lecturers to give them feedback on their own performance and to point out what they are doing well as well as how they can improve.

 You are a demonstrator and notice that a large group of students all seem to have made the same mistake in their write-up this week. You think they are copying without understanding. You know that some of their experiments failed in the session and they were very worried about not having any results. What can you do?

Failing to get results

This is such a common problem that most practicals have made provision for this in some way, providing or sharing a set of results. Students may need you to emphasise that practicals are not just about results and to focus on the process as well as the product.

Copying

Demonstrators need to draw such issues to the notice of the lecturer in charge of the practical work as soon as possible. The lecturer has options about how to deal with this depending on the stage of the course, any previous history, and so on. Copying can often be a sign of pressure on the students and weaknesses in the assessment practices. In both cases it is important for the lecturer to emphasise the importance of avoiding plagiarism in any scientific work to the whole group. If some are copying, others are allowing their work to be copied. See Chapter 3 for a note on plagiarism.

 FURTHER READING

Allison, I. (1995) 'Demonstrating', in F. Forster, D. Hounsell and S. Thompson (eds) *Tutoring and Demonstrating: A Handbook*, Sheffield: CVCP UCoSDA. There are some pointers here and some examples of feedback sheets. There may well be useful information for your situation in other chapters, not specifically aimed at lab work.

Birnie, J. and Mason O'Connor, K. (1998) *Practicals and Laboratory Work in Geography*, Gloucester: Geography Disciplines Network. A very positively reviewed series of guides to discipline-based practice.

Brown G., Bull, J. and Pendlebury, M. (1997) 'Assessing Practical Work', in *Assessing Student Learning in Higher Education*, London: Routledge. A useful chapter with suggestions about diversifying assessment, for example, using posters for formative and summative assessment.

 WEB SITE

http://dbweb.liv.ac.uk/ltsnpsc/default.htm

The LTSN Physical Sciences web site has begun to compile a resource database of practicals and there are an increasing number of case studies on line.

Chapter 9

Assessing problem classes and problem-based learning

INTRODUCTION

This chapter focuses on some of the issues involved in assessing students working in a problem- or enquiry-based way. Such classes might be common in engineering and mathematically based courses, supporting applications of numerical work in economics or geography. Increasingly, problem-based approaches are being used to support work in other knowledge-dominated subjects, such as problem-based learning techniques used in the medical curriculum. These techniques are being adapted and applied in engineering contexts where team work and processes of defining and solving problems are being assessed as well as the results and calculations. Computer-based assessment is becoming an important way of identifying and developing students' mathematical abilities outside of contact time. See Chapter 3 for definitions and some examples of sources of software.

Demonstrating and the marking of coursework play an important part in the undergraduate teaching of engineering students, especially in the formative first and second years of the undergraduate provision. Typically lecture group sizes are large and example classes serve as a direct point of contact with module teaching staff. Ideally, such classes should act to provide a bridge to independent study and instilling confidence, helping students to consolidate the topics and techniques they have learned in lectures, tutorials or through reading textbooks.

MATHEMATICAL ABILITY – VARIATIONS

In all engineering courses a level of mathematical ability is required. However, any large class will include a spectrum of qualifications and attitudes. A careful survey of first year engineering degree students at Warwick University by C.T. Shaw and V.F. Shaw was able to identify six distinct groups and their associated profiles.

The analysis showed the six clusters are:

- *The High Flyers.* These are A-level students with mathematics grades A or B, who have always enjoyed mathematics and always found it easy.
- *The Downhillers.* These are A-level students with grades A, B, C or D, who come from comprehensive schools or Sixth Form Colleges. Previously they enjoyed mathematics and found it easy, but now they hate mathematics and find it difficult. They have little motivation but a strong desire to improve.
- *The Averages.* They are A-level students with grades A, B, C, or D or BTEC Level iv students. To them everything seems average but they still want to improve.
- *The Haters.* They are A-level students with grades C or D or BTEC students of all levels. They have always found mathematics difficult and have never enjoyed it. They have little motivation and no wish to improve.
- *The Realistics.* They are A-level students with grades A, B or C or BTEC Level iv students. For them mathematics is now more difficult and less enjoyable. Even though the workload is heavy, they have some motivation and are keen to improve.
- *The Outliers.* This group consists of students who do not fall into the previous categories, possibly because of special background studies or experiences or expectations.

The proportions of students within these groups may differ, but the basic groupings are apposite. For reference, the number of students recorded at Warwick were High Flyers (14 per cent), Downhillers (9 per cent), Averages (27 per cent), Haters (22 per cent), Realistics (26 per cent) and Outliers (1 student).

By performing further analysis on the cluster groups, the following associated group profiles were discernible:

- *The High Flyers.* These students found the course notes useful, the textbook excellent and the tutors average. For them most topics are not difficult.

- *The Downhillers*. These students did not find the course notes, textbook and tutors useful. In the main, they found the topics to be of average difficulty or slightly difficult.
- *The Averages*. These students found the course notes, textbook and tutor to be useful. For them all topics are of average difficulty.
- *The Haters*. These students found the course notes and textbook to be of little use, but they found the tutors to be average.
- *The Realistics*. They found the course notes to be poor, the textbook to be good and the tutors to be excellent. They found all topics to be of average difficulty.

Knowledge of these different groupings highlight that different strategies may be required in dealing with student queries and assessment. It is important to realise that quantitative skills is only one element of an engineering education. For numerous students achieving a bare pass or resit pass in mathematics, say, may not be an undue hindrance to a successful engineering career.

Visiles and audiles

Most engineering students learn and think by using visual means supplemented by words, rather than by aural means supplemented by diagrams, pictures and 3D models (Figure 9.1).

■ **FIGURE 9.1**
Visiles and audiles

There are three other points which need to be considered in relation to effective learning. First, and obviously, a knowledge base is necessary for understanding. However, there is evidence that the way in which knowledge is acquired can inhibit or enhance understanding. Problem-centred approaches appear to produce more flexible learning networks which are more readily applied to new problems. Second, the knowledge–understanding continuum is not a dichotomy. At one extreme of the knowledge-seeking style there is the learning and reproduction of isolated facts, but at the other is the handling and management of knowledge. This end of reproductive learning merges imperceptibly into understanding. Third, the student's own predispositions and early experience of the subject draw out different styles of learning. A deep learner in Mechanical Engineering might become a nervous surface learner in Modern Poetry and vice versa.

Effective learning is most likely to occur:

- when the structure and learning tasks used build upon earlier learning;
- when the students develop their repertoire of skills from direct teaching, explicit modelling, practice, feedback, and reflection on their own approaches;
- when the students can take responsibility for their own learning, when they have some freedom of choice, when they are encouraged and trained in self-assessment and when they have opportunities to explore alternative approaches;
- when the contract of learning is conducive to active engagement in learning;
- when the students perceive that effort leads to success and its recognition.

PROBLEM-SOLVING STRATEGIES

Example classes provide an invaluable link between the concentrated delivery of material in lectures and students' private attempts to understand and reproduce the taught techniques. Such classes also give students opportunities to work interactively with their peers and with a member of the teaching staff. Such classes also provide students with the chance to take some responsibility for their own learning – an opportunity sadly missed by some.

In mathematics, the natural sciences and engineering, the subject matter is characterised by strong logical threads, which in turn leads to a fairly strict sequential presentation. Students are exposed to a hierarchical structure or a series of stepping stones, where failure to understand one topic can prejudice their chances of coping adequately with later topics which build on it. Hence, an individual with a 'mental block' on a topic, especially one near the start of the course, can quickly land in difficulties.

The present section focuses on classes dealing particularly with problem solving. A key idea is that problem solving is a skill that needs to be acquired by application and practice and fine tuned with experience and cannot be readily 'learnt' from reading lecture notes, or even model solutions.

Developing strategies

Rather than tell students about different approaches to problem solving it is better to ask them to describe how they do it and then summarise various approaches which they and you use. A common approach is the five-pronged attack.

1   Have I met a similar problem before?
2   What is the nub of the problem?
3   What approaches can I use?
4   What should I do when I get stuck?
5   How should I check the solution?

Each of these questions need unpacking further and the approach may be non-linear. One can work backwards from a solution or estimated solution; one can start in the middle and work outwards; one can change or simplify variables or hold a variable constant or one can try to invent a simpler version of the problem and tackle that as a preliminary.

Another approach, developed by Don Woods, Department of Chemical Engineering, McMaster University, is:

0   I can – the motivation step.
1   Define – draw a figure, list known and unknowns etc.
2   Explore – think about it, is it a routine problem, is it a problem in a problem etc.?

3   Plan – set up the steps or flowchart, use formal/mathematical logic or procedural steps.
4   Do it – put in the values.
5   Check – for errors in reasoning and number crunching, check against external criteria.
6   Generalise – how did I do it? How could it be done more effectively? What can be ignored, etc.?

Novices ignore step 1, rush step 2, ignore step 3, tend to ignore step 5 and rarely do step 6, unless specifically asked to do so. They often try to start with 3 and 4 combined and then get stuck.

All of these strategies and many more will be familiar to you.

Structured examples

Structured examples are given to students for numerous reasons that include:

- They help the learning process.
- They encourage students to keep pace with material – if the material is structured hierarchically, it is particularly difficult to catch up and grasp new material at the same time.
- They can be diagnostic, helping students to assess their progress, demonstrators to assess where help is particularly needed and the course team to assess the success of the teaching.
- They may be instructional, for example, using a problem, the solution to which enhances the students' grasp of the subject.
- They often provide a contact point between the tutor and the group or even individual students – it can suggest where tutorial discussion should commence.
- They may contribute to the overall assessment.

There are various common problems in dealing with coursework that may be anticipated in advance. It is important that all markers know and understand the assessment criteria and the marking scheme in use for the relevant module. This is usually accomplished by each marker receiving a carefully written full solution to the exercises, possibly with annotations to indicate where alternative approaches to the solutions are acceptable. Markers should also be prepared to ask module staff for

127

detailed explanations of ambiguities in the marking criteria. Where several markers are involved in joint marking of a module then it is often sensible for some ongoing discussions between these markers to maintain a consistency. It is the students' responsibility to do the exercises and helpful feedback is expected, but it is not the marker's role to replace lack of effort by the student, however well intentioned.

Figure 9.2 shows a job assessment sheet for problem classes.

 IN THE DISCIPLINES

Every year I assess hundreds of questions for one of the national exam boards in Physics. The mark scheme is well worked out and it should be absolutely straightforward. Usually it is, but I still need to be able to use my judgement and my subject knowledge to decide when a student deserves marks for their attempt and when they don't. This makes quite a difference to their final classification sometimes.

(Physics lecturer)

I can't help feeling that they shouldn't be here if they don't love the subject and want to do it themselves. I tend to have very high expectations and have to remember to support the weaker students in the assessment process as well as challenge the best ones. I used to make all the problems challenging for them, but I manage to restrict myself to just one or two now and I make sure I label them as extra-challenging questions so that all levels can achieve something.

(Economics lecturer)

PROBLEM SCENARIOS

 You notice that a group of friends are making identical errors in your problem. You think they are copying without understanding. What do you do?

Like most potential plagiarism problems, this depends to a small extent on where in the course it occurs. Plagiarism in regular large volume work such as reports and problem solving usually occurs when students do not really understand the purpose of their efforts, have no clear idea of what a good response would look like and no grasp of the overall method which is being reached for. Refer to definitions of plagiarism

Assessment	Third year problems in economics
Content	Level 2, time series analysis
Style	Show workings, complete prepared sheet.
Previous experience	Attended lecture Students – first introduction to this tricky subject.
Anticipate problems	Increasing difficulty. Expect all to attempt 1–6.
Who & stage	Final year, final term.
How many	45
How much	10 problems
Time per script	5–7 minutes
Criteria/mark scheme	Dept.coursework classification A–F, model answers.
Formative	General encouraging feedback required, particularly for those who are struggling. Tick sheet for problem-solving method, with pre-prepared comments.
Summative	Small role – 10% of module is assessed problem class work.
Plan for feedback	Ten minutes at start of next problem class, to compare with model answer and diagnose own mistakes and explain to a peer.
Plan to check standards	Compare table of results with expected norms.
Sampling	
Any additions	
Assessment plan	
Preparation	Photocopy model answers, one for each student, with space for comment.
Initial sampling	
Session 1	10 problem sheets – brief personal comment as I go. 60 minutes. Mini break.
Session 2	15 problems: 60 minutes. Break 20 mins.
Session 3	20 reports: 60 minutes
Record grades, submit, make copy	
Remember for next time	Give them revision notes and worked example reference to text at head of problem sheet.
Issues to report to assessment organiser	Clarify mark scheme for exam, my questions might be too hard – check standards.
Issues to report to students	
Any other comments	Mix up abilities in class more – good students tend to work together.

FIGURE 9.2 Job assessment sheet: worked example for problem class

and ensure that students are clear how they apply in your discipline area. Reinforce this with encouragement and penalties; use the carrot and the stick.

 You have a very large problem-solving class of first years. You read through the first question of the first ten and they all make basic errors. The mathematical ability seems to vary enormously. What do you do?

Mathematical ability will always vary within a group. Encourage students to assess their own ability and suggest managable strategies for each cluster. Provide revision and practical tools for students to practise, there are some computer-based packages which can help. Make sure you are familiar with what is available through investigating what other colleagues in the discipline have found and displayed on the LTSN (Learning and Teaching Subject Network) sites for your disciplines.

Perhaps in class you can try to mix groups to spread out abilities. Get some students to explain concepts to others – good for revision and spreads your effort around. Find ways to be positive and encouraging and keep your efforts realistic and build over the longer term. Focus on method and effort and practice rather than just feedback of the wrong answers. Teach and use a consistent method of problem solving which each can refer to and use when they get stuck or struggle. Give positive reinforcement to all efforts to identify and use these stages in your feedback.

 Your PBL (problem-based learning) class is being very ably led by one student in the role of chair. You notice that two students are not participating. Do you intervene? How will you assess their contribution?

Systems vary, sometimes your formative feedback will be welcome to the individuals. You might be required to assess their contributions. Seek clarification from the PBL convenor.

You could structure some reflection on process and contribution at the end of each session using prompt questions, or giving your observations if appropriate. If you judge the problem is extreme and the students are struggling, report your observations to the convenor or tutor to help them support the students effectively in the light of their overall contribution, just as you would report on non-attendance.

 You spend each class working very hard to get the students to develop their problem-solving skills which you have given them a hand-out on in week one. They prefer to get you to work – what do you do next session?

Where students are constantly ignoring an important aspect of work and taking no notice of your feedback, it may be time to change your strategy.

Perhaps start each class with working through a problem – use your problem-solving framework consistently. Devise some tasks which focus on this aspect, for example, not solving a problem but labelling the steps; do different sections of the problem; divide a problem between groups and set them to hand on a problem to the next group to do the next stages; get students to complete partial solutions. Vary this. Encourage them to use the framework with each other. Ensure your demonstrators do the same thing. Give high marks in assessment to this aspect to underline how important it is to you and them.

Encouraging attendance for all students

 All your students hand in their work on time but attendance in class is rapidly dropping in your problem-solving classes where you provide feedback on their work. You notice that many of the students who are not coming are your 'average' students. You spend all your time with 'favourite' very keen students who are keen to learn more and with students who seem to need you to do all the work and hand in very poor work and never seem to improve. Is this a problem?

Yes, this can be a problem. Students will 'vote with their feet' and attend things which they see as important. It could be that you are not contributing to their grades or assessment in any way. Feedback the attendance question and your concerns to the appropriate colleague for future evaluation. You cannot force students to attend but you can make sure the course resources match the needs of students and are not wasteful.

One tip might be to re-structure the social groupings during the class so that some able students are matched with weaker, more passive students. This can enhance the learning achieved by both. Keep changing the small groups you establish regularly to minimise patterns which are not working well.

To encourage attendance, you could return student work in class. Perhaps split the session into two halves so that students who don't want to stay for the whole thing stay for some and that you can focus on working with the weaker students, perhaps as a group to maximise your input (saying things once to the whole group) then using small group teaching methods (see Exley and Dennick 2004) to ensure students participate.

Your role is to divide up your time and responsibility equitably between as many students as possible. Inevitably, where attendance is not compulsory, some students may decide they have better ways to spend their time. I believe there is a problem when the average student is not gaining from a situation, as these are the majority of our students.

 Student attendance at problem classes has dropped significantly. What can you do?

On the understanding that we do not plan to spend time needlessly delivering teaching, it might be a good idea to plan sessions so that all students can gain from attending sessions and it is worth pointing this out to them and asking for information from them as to what would be the most appropriate support.

Monitor your time and attention during the class. Are your favourites sitting at the front and engaging your attention? Try altering the pattern of seating in the room, or hand out colour codes to randomise groups to spread the pattern anew. The new pattern will have its own imbalances and unfairness, but they will be different and may cancel out the prevailing previous one. Tell the class what you are doing, that your time is rationed, and you are aiming to work with each group once before you can move on to work with the same group again. Approach people who are avoiding you. Join the group and sit quietly. Ask innocuous questions in order to encourage.

Think up new ways to motivate students who do attend. Offer special exam-orientated briefings at the start to encourage people to attend.

Take a register, no need to tell students what you intend to do with the information, you may choose to do nothing. Offer prizes and set competitions with smaller easier puzzles at the start of the session to encourage people to limber up and so all can potentially contribute. Encourage those who have found the solution to move on to work with groups who haven't found the solution yet and help them along.

Try to ensure that you check how each student is progressing. Avoid favouritism and be wary of being drawn into spending excessive time on any one student or small group of students. Interact more with students. Enquire of students about their progress; questions such as 'Is everything OK?' will invite the non-committal 'Yes', often because the student may be reluctant to admit they are stuck. More inviting questions such as 'What question are you on?' can lead to a more meaningful exchange for you to gauge the level of progress. It is important to discourage students from leaving early; students leaving will often generate a 'herd' effect where those around will give up and join those who have left. However, students not wishing to participate in the class should be encouraged to leave immediately; such students will inevitably disturb others who may be in need of assistance.

 FURTHER READING

Brown, G., Bull, J. and Pendlebury, M. (1997) *Assessing Student Learning in Higher Education*, London: Routledge.
    There is a useful chapter, 'Assessing Problem Classes' which further addresses concerns.

Chapter 10

Assessing in examinations

INTRODUCTION

The message of this chapter is essentially a summary of everything which has gone before. In examinations, your role is to ensure that you operate assessment to the highest levels that you can; in setting the tests, in summatively assessing tests, in managing the strict timescales and numbers of staff involved with sufficient checks in place to ensure optimal fairness. In essence, like a competitive race, an exam requires the assessor (as well as the assessed) to apply their skills in a limited time to a situation which has been known about for the whole course.

Many disciplines are moving away from reliance on examinations as the major summative device. It is now unusual for examinations to be the only method of deciding the results of a course. However, exams continue to play an important role as their strengths may well combine advantages for staff as well as certain types of students. For example, many have speculated that exams have been shown to favour strategic, risk-taking students who respond well to pressure and may not be able to keep up consistently high results throughout the time of the course. Today's students have many other considerations in their lives; perhaps working full- or part-time, having family and caring responsibilities which might suit periods of intense concentration infrequently, rather than continual assessment.

What are the skills and abilities that an unseen written exam tests?

- time management
- stress tolerance
- writing skills
- memory
- knowledge.

Figure 10.1 is a draft taxonomy which compares the wide variety of examination styles for their potential to test levels and types of learning and suggests where staff have concerns which may need to be monitored closely.

Figure 10.2 shows a job assessment sheet for example exam questions.

There are guidelines within institutions to encourage management of concerns about the examinations process. Below is a note on some codes of practice for examinations, Queen Mary, University of London, November 2001.

1 Code of Practice on double marking

1.1 The primary objective of double marking is to confirm the standard of marking: to ensure that all the assessments have been considered thoroughly, conscientiously and objectively, and that the method of assessment complies with the marking scheme approved by the examination board. This is becoming increasingly important with the pressures upon staff, both in relation to the volume of scripts to be considered, and the short timescale for completion of the process. A secondary advantage is a guard against conscious or unconscious discrimination towards an individual student.

1.2 The College has adopted the following policy with regard to double marking:

Examination Scripts

1.3 All examination scripts that count towards student progression and/or classification for Honours must be double marked by one of the following procedures –

[a] Independent assessment of the script by two examiners, where neither sees the comments or marks of the other until the whole procedure has been completed ('blind' double marking).

[b] Assessment of the scripts by two examiners, where the second examiner is able to see the comments and marks made by the first examiner ('open' double marking).

[c] In mathematically-based disciplines which have a detailed marking scheme which allows little or no discretion to the examiner, the second examiner checks that all sections of the script have been marked, and that the marks have been correctly totalled.

135

This taxonomy compares examination styles as regards their potential to test levels of learning of different kinds. It makes a number of assumptions which are based largely on experience, but which seem to be generally valid. However, it is possible to change the values given under 'potential for assessment' of some items in the taxonomy by the careful design of questions.

Categories under examination

- **Knowledge** means information which has been memorised and can be recalled.
- **Skills I** means skills that can be judged fairly objectively - like maths calculations, spelling, grammar, computer skills, planning, etc.
- **Skills II** means skills that require judgement by the examiners - like communication skills (written or oral), interpersonal skills, leadership skills, etc.
- **Reliability** refers to the likelihood of different examiners giving the same mark.
- **Robustness** refers to the resistance of the method to abuse by students (e.g. by cheating, plagiarism, unauthorised group activity, etc.).
- **Understanding** refers to aspects of deep processing (ability to integrate experience and the task, and to apply knowledge to problem solving).

Type of assessment	Potential for assessment		Staff concerns	

1 Closed book exam – type A

Descriptive	Skills 1	**	Staff time	**
Derivative	Skills II	*	Reliability	***
Numerical problems	Understanding	*	Robustness	***
Choice allowed	Knowledge	***		

Notes: Conventional exam. Favours strategic learners. Testing of understanding can be improved by careful design of questions.

2 Closed book exam – type B

Interpretation of evidence	Skills 1	***	Staff time	***
Role play	Skills II	***	Reliability	**
	Understanding	***	Robustness	***
No choice allowed	Knowledge	***		

Notes: Demands more assessment effort by staff than exam type A.

3 Open book exam

	Skills 1	***	Staff time	**
	Skills II	**	Reliability	***
	Understanding	*??	Robustness	***
	Knowledge	*		

Notes: Tests ability to access information and model answers to problems. The method primarily relaxes demands on memory. Some claim this kind of exam tests understanding well.

4 Short answer examination

	Skills 1	**	Staff time	*
	Skills II	*	Reliability	***
	Understanding	*	Robustness	***
	Knowledge	***		

Notes: Useful for testing a wide range of topics in one exam. Little opportunity for students to show flair.

FIGURE 10.1 A draft taxonomy of assessment styles

Type of assessment	Potential for assessment		Staff concerns	

5 Objective tests

Multi-choice	Skills 1	***	Staff time	*
True/false	Skills II	*	Reliability	***
Matching	Understanding	*	Robustness	**
Completion	Knowledge	***		

Notes: Vulnerable to successful guesswork unless errors are negatively scored. Gives no opportunity for students to show flair.

6 Practical exams

Lab experiment or computer design task	Skills 1	***	Staff time	**
Computer simulation	Skills II	*	Reliability	**
Observation	Understanding	**	Robustness	***
	Knowledge	**		

Notes: Difficult to handle large student numbers.

7 Oral examinations

Individual viva	Skills 1	*	Staff time	***
Presentation to audience	Skills II	***	Reliability	**
	Understanding	***	Robustness	***
	Knowledge	**		

Notes: Difficult to handle large student numbers. Can be used to check borderline grading decisions, or as a random check. Individual viva is stressful for students; widely used abroad for a finals assessment. At 20 minutes per student, covering more than one course, this is not necessarily excessively time-consuming. Requires examiners with special expertise.

8 Course work assignments

Written assignments	Skills 1	***	Staff time	***
Presentation to audience	Skills II	***	Reliability	**
	Understanding	***	Robustness	*
	Knowledge	*		

Notes: Educationally valuable, especially for developing understanding and skills, but open to plagiarism and abuse.

9 Projects

Individual project	Skills 1	***	Staff time	***
Group project	Skills II	***	Reliability	**
	Understanding	***	Robustness	*
	Knowledge	*		

Notes: Educationally valuable, but there is conflict between roles of tutors as guides and assessors. Group projects less robust, but educationally more valuable.

10 Peer assessment or self-assessment

Of projects	Skills 1	***	Staff time	*
Of assignments	Skills II	***	Reliability	**
	Understanding	***	Robustness	**
	Knowledge	*		

Notes: Strongly motivating and valuable for teaching understanding. Requires skilled management. Possibility of exploitation by students, not generally borne out in practice

EPC (March 1992)

Assessment	Short answer Essay Q'S.
Content	Key concepts: osmosis, transpiration; key terminology, 10 terms, limitations of current models, experimental data, compares different plant models.
Essay style	250 word limit, exam conditions, penalise poor expression, spellings, notes by maximum of 20%.
Previous experience	Normal mark distribution expected. A few may fail the assessment at this stage, few good.
Anticipate problems	Expect they will find this question fairly straightforward, expect half will choose this one.
Who & stage	First year's biological sciences; plant systems.
How many	55 [check policy −1 missed exam through illness]
How much	250 words max Approx one page
Time per essay	3–5 minutes
Criteria/Mark scheme	Adapted from dept general essay scheme + 90% content. PASS – to 2nd year – not degree classification.
Formative	Predictive of degree classification.
Summative	Grades reported to module convenor, copy to departmental secretary – 2 days, return hard copy of results plus scripts.
Plan for feedback	10 mins with personal tutor at start of year – use feedback summary sheet to inform.
Plan to check standards	Anonymous marking, compare with results in other modules, prior to exam board . . .
Sampling	Start and end.
Any additions	
Assessment plan	
Preparation	Put into numerical order in folder one, spreadsheet entry for each student, model answer ready, brief feedback sheet for each.
Session 1	
Initial sampling	Read, 5, 17, 25, 40, and 53 for initial sample of range. 25 minutes. Assess 10 questions, initial grades given, put into folder 2 in grade order. Short break – notes on common issues, misunderstandings of question, etc. for examination report. 60 minutes
Session 2	Assess 20 questions – 60 mins. Add to notes.
Session 3	Assess 25 questions – 60 mins. Add to notes.
Session 4	Re-assess borderlines 30 minutes. Re-assess one from each grade category. Analyse spreadsheet for normal distribution. Word process examiner report from notebook: 60 minutes

Record grades, submit, make copy, handover

Remember for next time

Issues to report to assessment organiser Submit examiner report

Issues to report to students Feedback sheets to personal tutors with grades

Any other comments

■ **FIGURE 10.2** Job assessment sheet: worked example for exam questions

1.4 The examination board must have a procedure whereby the comments and marks of the two examiners can be distinguished (for example, by using different coloured ink), and each examiner must write the total marks allocated, and his/her initials on the cover sheet to the scripts.

<u>Coursework</u>

1.4 Pieces of coursework that count more than 25% towards the final mark for a unit of module must be double marked in the same way as examination scripts.

1.5 Assessed coursework that counts less than 25% towards the final mark for a unit is not required to be double marked, but the Examination Board must have a procedure for monitoring the quality of the marking. This is particularly important in units assessed wholly by coursework where no individual item contributes more than 25% towards the overall mark, and there is therefore no requirement for any double marking.

THE ROLE OF FORMATIVE FEEDBACK IN EXAMINATIONS

The good news is that you will not be required to feedback detailed written advice and suggestions to students about their performance. However, it is increasingly seen as good practice to review performance with all students except for those due to leave your institution. You might find it helpful to use your usual methods of indicating to yourself on the script what your judgement is about a student's work in assisting you to arrive at your summative judgement. You may also wish to adapt your usual feedback sheets in order to record and justify your judgements of student levels of achievement in a way that will allow you to refer back to it easily when you are collating the results of many students and sampling for the soundness of your assessments at each level.

The exam regulations at Queen Mary, University of London have the following to say on this matter.

1.1 Request for review of an exam board decision

11.1 Examination board business is confidential and members MUST NOT speak to students about their detailed performance. (This does not, of course, prevent tutors or advisers discussing with students, in general terms, those areas in which their performance was unsatisfactory.)

THE ROLE OF FEEDBACK ON EXAMINERS

It is good practice to publish and make available the examiners' response to the students' achievements. For example, the London School of Hygiene and Tropical Medicine publish the examination paper and the examiners' report, question by question, which is then made available to both staff and subsequent students. The commentary highlights the performance of students, concepts which were ill-understood by significant numbers of students, and where questions may have misled or been difficult for all students.

SOME ISSUES IN EXAMINATIONS

Disability

During examinations it is particularly important to be able to accommodate the needs of all students. Here is precept 13 of the QAA (Quality Assurance Agency), the government body responsible for ensuring standards in higher education:

> Assessment and exam policies, practices and procedures should provide disabled students with the same opportunities as their peers to demonstrate the achievement of learning outcomes.

This may entail detailed planning and flexibility in the enforcement of policies at the institutional level. Make sure you know where to ensure you and your students have access to the best advice. Most institutions do now employ advisers who have specialist expertise in this area. For more information, the LTSN Assessment Series booklet number eight provides a briefing on how assessment issues impact on disabled students.

A useful web address for exam stress is: http://www.ad.ic.ac.uk/healthcentre/examain.htm.

IN THE DISCIPLINES

For the Human Communication and Deafness Group at the University of Manchester, scripts may often be marked by professionals external to the school. The following extract is taken from their web site which explains procedural matters to do with exam marking, called Redtape:

Procedure

For each question on each script, the first marker will write their mark in pencil in the first column and write their initials next to it. The second marker will consider this when moderating this mark.

The first marker will then select a sample of papers for the second marker to look at (usually high, medium, low and any fails/problematic cases) and will supply an outline of what they expect in the answer to each question.

The second marker should initial the first marker's mark if s/he agrees with it, or write in pencil a second mark and his/her own initials.

After discussion, the agreed final mark should then be written in ink. (The reasons for the mark plus initial is that sometimes on scripts which are made up of several marks and then are changed by second and external, it is very difficult to judge which mark is the final agreed mark.)

When all marks have been discussed in this way, the first marker opens the scripts and matches up the library numbers with names and will then ensure final marks are on all papers in ink, and that these marks are then transcribed onto a sheet with names. The first marker will then indicate on this sheet which scripts should be sent to the external. Again this is usually a selection of high, medium and low fails, plus the whole of one question. Please write the external a note to include with the scripts and mark sheet.

The secretary will then bind up the packages and send them off via the security mail system.

When the marks and comments have been returned to the first marker, please ensure that any changes in marks are shown clearly. Please also give the letter from the external to the secretary for her records.

Note: Where the first marker is external to the centre, the internal marker should open all the scripts.

Such detail is very helpful when dealing with such important documents. The practices will vary but seek advice for your centre.

> Getting ready for the exam board is terribly hard work and pretty boring. I have to have absolutely everything there to support any discussion which might crop up – even though it usually doesn't. Administration is not an academic's top priority and I couldn't do this without the help of the administrators and secretaries who coordinate the whole process for our department. They are excellent.
>
> (Senior Lecturer, Engineering)

Here a new lecturer in business management comments on her first exam assessing experience:

> I had 300 scripts to assess but it was much easier than the first essay question I set for them at the end of semester one. Their answers to the questions were shorter and more to the point and I had a much clearer idea of exactly what I was looking for. I also expected it to take a lot of time – and it did, but at least I was prepared.

PROBLEM SCENARIOS

 The external examiner says your question is too hard. What do you do?

Define hard? Too hard for most of the students? Too big a jump to be able to differentiate between different levels of achievement? Too much of a trick, narrow question? Get advice. Try to break the essence of the question down into stages which you can be confident that most students will be able to achieve if they have attended most of the course. Seek advice from your experienced colleagues. See if one of your demonstrators, tutorial assistants, your best student could complete something similar in exam conditions. If they struggle, the external examiner is right.

Beware of having too high expectations of student performance in exams. Arrange to see some real exam papers which give evidence of what is normally expected of each level of student. Exam papers are not a time to make mistakes. Checks and balances exist to help you avoid this. Do not be proud or challenging at exam time. That is not the intention.

The module convenor says he doesn't find mark schemes very useful and that you can make it up as you go along. What do you do?

This response may still be common in areas where individuality is still prized, perhaps in specialist arts and humanities areas where people are used to working mainly alone. This would be unlikely to occur in an area of large cooperatively taught and assessed curriculum, such as medicine or chemistry. However, once you have attempted to get as much debriefing information as you can from your convenor, I recommend that you look further afield among more sympathetic colleagues perhaps, checking in the exam regulations, finding out as much about the cooperation with the external examiner as possible. Construct your own mark scheme, which I'm sure the convenor may well have a similar version of in their head. Decide how you are going to weight the marks that you allocate against the criteria that you set. If you are using short essays, or short answers, depending on your discipline, you may be willing to allocate most of the marks for content which is expressed legibly, and not deduct marks for students giving their information as bullet points, or in a form that contains spelling errors or mistakes.

In subjects where the form of expression is central to the nature of the content, decide your maximum penalties and threshold levels of expectation at each of the degree classifications. This approach should be familiar to you from your coursework marking. Perhaps you will need to revise your expectations downwards for what students are able to produce in exam conditions. Even able students will lack their usual focus and polish in exam conditions. Confer with colleagues to define what you believe to be fair and consistent for assessing unfinished essays, plan only, or extra marks for flair in such circumstances.

Students are doing your paper last of all. You think the exam board will be the following week and you are best man at your friend's wedding during the weekend between. What do you do?

Your time and priority management skills are being put to the test here. It may be possible to influence the speed with which the papers get to you. Are they being double marked? Could you go first? Can you impress on the other people involved that you need to have the best amount of time available? Plan your other activities to prioritise your availability for this assessment task. Complete as much as possible of all your other tasks on these days. There is no point leaving shopping and writing your speech for the same time as well.

Prepare in advance

Prepare all your paperwork, job assessment sheets, model answers, prepared mark sheets in advance. Many exams are marked anonymously so you may need to sort out ID numbers as well. Ensure you are clear about where the results have to be handed in and in what form at the end of your stint.

Make time for the task

Ensure that you arrange adequate time for the task – inevitably, tasks which we haven't done before take longer than we expect. Use your best habits. Assess yourself regularly, are things going to plan? How could you change what you are doing for the better? Try to stay in one place – either work or home – for the whole task so that you minimise the chances of losing work in transit. Make a back-up copy of what you do and print it out. At least you don't have to give feedback. Spend time sampling and checking classifications instead until you are confident that you have identified the correct grade in most cases. Where you have doubts at the borderlines, signal this and arrange to confer appropriately with your co-marker to ensure you are confident, whatever is allowed within your guidelines. Good luck!

 You emailed the results and your feedback from your home to work. When you get into the office the secretary says she never got it. What can you do?

Naturally, you made a copy of this important email and information, or brought in the original rough draft. If you are unsuccessful at retrieving the information, if no one at home can re-send the information in time, you may have to re-construct it from the material you have available. There will be no sympathy for you in this situation. Always behave as if this is going to happen and you can never be caught out.

 You have a pile of exam scripts and a mark scheme. However, several students have come up with an excellent correct solution which is better, in your view, than the model answer provided by the module convenor – what can you do?

You can use your own judgement to re-allocate credit within the mark scheme offered by the convenor. After all, you are employed to use your judgement and assess according to what is valid, reliable and fair. However, be sure to alert the convenor to your actions and ensure that there is adequate documentation attached to the scripts and available in case the external examiner picks up the change and favours justification for the operation of judgement in such circumstances. It is only likely to affect a small proportion of students, probably more able ones. In this case, other exam performances will amply demonstrate their ability. However, even quite small discrepancies could come to hold extra weight if someone is at the borderline between different classification or if there is felt to be large consequence as a result, for example of awarding a first or failing someone. Your information could turn out to be relevant and you may not be present to provide the information.

FURTHER READING

McCarthy, D. and Hurst, A. (2001) *A Briefing on Assessing Disabled Students* Available from the LTSN website at: http://www.ltsn.ac.uk/application. asp?app=resources.asp&process=full_record&section=generic&id=8 accessed on 25 June 2003

A web site which explains how to use Cronbach's alpha coefficient using SPSS: http://www.ats.ucla.edu/stat/spss/faq/alpha.html

A new site which offers students a range of resources including tips on examinations. It includes brief uncritical selections of resources at web sites offered by universities around the country and offers a 'lecturers' zone': http://www.palgrave.com/skills4study/html/resources.htm

References

Arthur, D. (1995) 'Problem-Solving Classes', in F. Forster, D. Hounsell and S. Thompson (eds) *Tutoring and Demonstrating: A Handbook*, Sheffield: CVCP UCoSDA.

Bean, J. C. (2001) *Engaging Ideas: The Professor's Guide to Integrating Writing, Critical Thinking, and Active Learning in the Classroom*, San Francisco, CA: Jossey-Bass.

Bloom, B. S. (1965) *A Taxonomy of Educational Objectives Handbook I: Cognitive Domain*, 2nd edition, New York: McKay.

Brown, G., Bull, J. and Pendlebury, M. (1997) *Assessing Student Learning in Higher Education*, London, Routledge.

Brown, S., Rust, C. and Gibbs, G. (1994) *Strategies for Diversifying Assessment in Higher Education*, Oxford: Oxford Centre for Staff Development.

Carroll, J. (2002) *A Handbook for Deterring Plagiarism in Higher Education* Oxford: Oxford Centre for Staff and Learning Development.

Covey, S. (1990) *The Seven Habits of Highly Effective People*, New York: Simon & Schuster Adult Publishing Group.

Cox, S. (1994) *Report Writing*, Coventry: Enterprise Capability Workshops, Coventry University.

Evison, A. (2002) 'Responding to Student Writing' unpublished presentation available at: http://www.learndev.qmul.ac.uk/elss/responding.pdf, accessed 25 June 2003.

Exley, K. and Dennick, R. (2004) *Small Group Teaching*, London: RoutledgeFalmer.

Graal, M. and Clark, R. (eds) (2000) *Writing Development in Higher Education: Partnerships across the Curriculum*, Leicester: Teaching and Learning Unit, University of Leicester.

Habeshaw, S., Gibbs, G. and Habeshaw, T. (1993a) *53 Interesting Ways to Assess your Students*, Bristol: Technical and Educational Services Ltd.

Habeshaw, S., Gibbs, G. and Habeshaw, T. (1993b) *53 Problems with Large Classes*, Bristol: Technical and Educational Services Ltd.

Haswell R. H. (1983) 'Minimal Marking', *College English* 45, 6: 166–70.

Higgins, R., Hartley, P. and Skelton, A. (2000) 'What Do Students Really Learn from Tutors' Comments?', in M. Graal and R. Clark *Writing Development in Higher Education*, Leicester: University of Leicester.

Hofstede, G. (1991) *Cultures and Organizations: Software of the Mind*, London: McGraw-Hill UK.

Hounsell, D. (1995) 'Marking and Commenting on Essays', in F. Forster, D. Hounsell and S. Thompson (eds) *Tutoring and Demonstrating: A Handbook*, Sheffield: CVCP UCoSDA.

Johnson, L. (1996) *Being an Effective Academic*, Oxford: Oxford Centre for Staff Development.

Kolb, D. A. (1984) *Experiential Learning: Experience as the Source of Learning and Development*, Englewood Cliffs, NJ: Prentice Hall.

Lewis, V. and Habeshaw, S. (1997) *Interesting Ways to Supervise Student Projects, Dissertations and Theses*, Bristol: Technical and Educational Services Ltd.

Menand, Louis (2000) *New Yorker* Magazine.

National Committee of Inquiry into Higher Education (1997) *Higher Education in the Learning Society, Report of the National Committee* (The Dearing Report) [online] (Chapter 9 'The Nature of Programmes', available at: http://www.ncl.ac.ujk.nciehe/nr130.htm).

Prestwich, K. N. (1998) 'Hawks and Doves Games Theory' in http://www.holycross.edu/departments/biology/kprestwi/behavior/ESS/HvD_intro.html, accessed 23 June 2003.

Ryan, J. (2000) *A Guide to Teaching International Students*, Oxford: Oxford Centre for Staff and Learning Development.

Spandell, V. and Stiggins, R. J. (1990) *Creating Writers: Linking Assessment and Writing Instruction*. Harlow: Longman.

Turner, D. (2002) *Designing and Delivering Modules*, Oxford: Oxford Centre for Staff and Learning Development.

From: Engineering Professors Conference 'Programme for the Improvement of the Quality Engineering Education', 5th workshop March 1992. (NB A first draft circulated for comment.)

Wakeford, R. (1999) 'Principles of Assessment', in H. Fry, S. Ketteridge, and S. Marshall (eds) *A Handbook for Teaching & Learning in Higher Education*, London: Kogan Page.

Washer, P. J. (2002) http://www.admin.qmul.ac.uk/esd/resource/briefings.htm for briefing papers written for academic staff at Queen Mary, University of London particularly Key Skills, accessed June 23 2003.

Whitton, A. A. and Cameron, K. S. (1991) *Developing Management Skills*, London: HarperCollins.

 ## WEB SITES

http://www.admin.qmul.ac.uk/registry/exam/index.shtml, accessed June 23 2003 current version, supersedes quoted version dated 2001.

http://www.seec-office.org.uk/. For details of publications on level descriptors and assessment.

http://www.thinkingwriting.qmul.ac.uk/help2.htm

http://www.jisc.ac.uk/mle/plagiarism

Index

eBooks – at www.eBookstore.tandf.co.uk

A library at your fingertips!

eBooks are electronic versions of printed books. You can store them on your PC/laptop or browse them online.

They have advantages for anyone needing rapid access to a wide variety of published, copyright information.

eBooks can help your research by enabling you to bookmark chapters, annotate text and use instant searches to find specific words or phrases. Several eBook files would fit on even a small laptop or PDA.

NEW: Save money by eSubscribing: cheap, online access to any eBook for as long as you need it.

Annual subscription packages

We now offer special low-cost bulk subscriptions to packages of eBooks in certain subject areas. These are available to libraries or to individuals.

For more information please contact webmaster.ebooks@tandf.co.uk

We're continually developing the eBook concept, so keep up to date by visiting the website.

www.eBookstore.tandf.co.uk